Dogalogue

Gill Capper

by

Gill Capper

HB

Honeybee Books

Honeybee Books

Published by Honeybee Books
Broadoak, Dorset
www.honeybeebooks.co.uk

ISBN: 978-1-910616-02-4

Gill Capper:
capperaphael@gmail.com

For Emil and Joe

Gill Capper is a journalist and poet living in Bridport, West Dorset. Last year she reached what used to be a pensionable age.

In the 1970's she was a founder member of the women's theatre group Cunning Stunts.

In 1985 she was a winner in the Cosmopolitan Journalist's Competition and for the next 20 years she worked as a freelance journalist, in London, for Cosmopolitan, She Magazine, The Evening Standard Magazine and, latterly, with a column on BBC Family Life in which she complained, with jokes, about life with teenage kids.

These days, after a decade lost to illness and romantic distractions, she keeps her hand in writing for Positive News, and writing and performing with Some Bridport Poets.

And now she has a dog…

"She writes without safety net" Julie Burchill

Contents

Prodogalogue..1

Cold Feet..3

Prep..5

All Systems Go..7

Meeting And Greeting..9

Maggie..11

Played Out..13

Fit As A Butcher's Dog..18

Puppy Parties..21

The Local Doggregation..24

Hector Untrained..26

Breaking Bed..29

Sons And Puppies..32

Counting The Ways I Love Thee..35

Doing The London Walk..38

The Dog's Dinner..41

Be Here-ish Now..44

To Do Or Not To Do..47

Achilles Heel..50

Reverting To Type..53

Ms Dolittle..56

Our Daily Dread   59

Teen Spirit   62

Anthropopwhadyamacallit   65

Duvet Days   68

On The Road Again   71

Procrastinations   74

A Fanny Festival   77

A Dog's Days In Wales   80

Going Swimmingly   84

After Glastonbury   87

Bad Hair Days   90

Dog Ends: An Epidogalogue   93

Prodogalogue

I have been on my own for five years. I am in recovery from a long relationship with a psycho. My children have left home. And recently I noticed myself experiencing inappropriate enjoyment from the body-search I got from the poker-faced lady at airport security check-in when my metal hip replacements set off the bleeping machine. "Don't stop", I thought, "Touch me. More!"

It's sad, I know. So desperate measures are called for. I have decided to get a dog. And I hope he turns out to be the loyal, faithful, unconditionally loving companion I have so spectacularly failed to find amongst mankind.

My puppy is currently growing in a nice warm kitchen in New Milton and he is the shape, size and consistency of a large *pain au chocolat*. I am going to call him Hector because I want him to be "gentle but bold and peace-loving" like his heroic namesake. But mostly because, despite his edibility, I do not want to call him a silly food name like the Mangos, Muffins, Marmites, Branstons and Rhubarbs of my acquaintance. (How undognified!)

My sister did once call a dog a classical name – Bucephalos – which sounded, hollered in the park, like a venereal disease, so Going to The Greek is not without its problems.

And there is another problem. As my friend Rose keeps gleefully pointing out, I don't like walking.

I am, however, already having fantasies about Hector licking my face to keep me conscious and barking like fuck to alert my neighbour Barry when I have the heart attack or stroke that my doctor promises me is inevitable if I continue to eat cheese and to refuse his blessed statins. So that's a positive.

Oh, I do hope I am not going to regret this...

Cold Feet

It is very interesting how people react when you tell them you are getting a dog. It falls into two categories. There are those who say, "Oh, a dog, how lovely, it will be your greatest joy, the light of your life, you'll wonder how you ever lived without one, everyone should have a dog".

Then there are the other ones. "Ooh, it's a lot of hard work, you know, a terrible tie. Are you sure you know what you are letting yourself in for? A Labrador? Ooh. Big dog. Lots of hair. Hope you haven't got any precious furniture, Ha Ha. Lots of walking. LOADS of walking. Rain or shine (and here they shake their doom-laden heads), you'll have to go out rain or shine…"

I'll give *them* a rain-or-shiner! (People *never* do this when you're having a baby!) It has been so disconcerting that I have been forced to develop a little Theory to help me contain my irritation. It goes like this: the people in the first category are happy with their lives and the people in the latter are not. So there!

I am not sure my self-serving little theory holds up because I have shied away from rigorously examining the evidence in case it isn't. But it jolly well feels good to run it through my mind whenever I get anxious about the possibility that I may NOT have thought this through and that it may just be me suffering from poor impulse control as usual, like the last sofa purchase which turned out not to be the sofa of my dreams.

Have I chosen the wrong *kind* of dog? Yesterday I saw a Farrow and Ball coloured Whippetty thing tripping down the road like an anorexic model on a catwalk. It had lovely slate grey/blue/white splodges on its coat in the shape of artists' palettes and it was truly distinctive. Is Hector going to be distinctive enough, I thought. Just an ordinary common or garden black lab. Perhaps if I get him one of those Oirish gypsy type rope leads he will look a bit more cool…

Forgive me, Hector, for being so shallow. I intend to become a better person for you, I do, I do…

Prep

I *think* I am prepared. But what a learning curve it has been. What an info overload. I have been on a dizzying number of dog sites in late night sessions of Doogling and my eyes have been opened. I had never heard of Cesar Millan, the "dog whisperer". Never heard of "clicker training". Never knew how many issh-oos there were in the dog world and with what positively canine ferocity these tugs of war are invested.

I've discovered toe-curling American forums where dog owners are called "mommies" and they talk about "going potty" all the time (and not in the English sense). There are whole websites devoted to recipes for stuffing Kongs – the world's favourite dog toy, apparently. (Frozen peanut butter, goats cheese and broccoli, anypup?) And who could fail to be seduced by the endless YouTube clips: "Amazing! 9 week old puppy plays the Arrival of the Queen of Sheba on the guitar!"

Then, what a heavenly retail fest! So far, being reliably middle class about this, I have bought two tasteful brown ceramic Mason and Cash dog bowls; some Bitter Apple spray to deter the chewing of the inherited Chippendale; a rubber nubbly thimble-shaped thingummy that fits on your finger for cleaning teeth; an ingenious dog lead that clicks into the car seat-belt connection; and a natural wheaten coloured undyed plaited chew ball that would not look out of place on the coffee table as a piece of Nautical Art.

I have eschewed all plastic. I have turned my snooty back on the garish day glo flashing squeaking bone shaped dog toys in This n That. I have refused the lure of dog treats containing sugar or E numbers. And I have filled my freezer with the products of Nurturing by Nature , a kind of doggie online farmers market which sells natural raw food dietary delicacies including blitzed fruit and vegetables, all delivered to your door in Chinese takeaway containers.

The only thing I have left to decide is whether to buy the Dizzy-Dog luxury faux suede dog bed or make do with a couple of old towels. I am deferring this decision until I have come to my senses and recalled my 1950's Northern thrifty no-nonsense commonsensical roots.

My brother-in-law has been overheard muttering, "you'd think nobody ever had a dog before" and I don't blame him. Really, dog-owning in the 21st century is a whole new ball game. I have definitely "gone par-dy".

All Systems Go

For the last three days even my cleaner Maggie has been sending me texts saying, "three more sleeps, two more sleeps, one more sleep…" And now Hector is here.

The first thing he did when he came into the house was pee on his bed. (Well, he didn't know it was his bed, did he?) Apart from that, he wasn't sick in the car, he didn't whine for more than a minute, he slept in his crate without a murmur until 5 o'clock in the morning when I was so excited to see him again I woke him up, ostensibly to pee, but actually to PLAY. Oh yes, I am in love all right. He is gorgeous.

But I am not going to go on in this cute-rifying manner. I have already broken one on my rules, namely, do not use soppy-lovers-bedroom-baby voice, even in private. And I *have* been: "Oo's my scrummy yummy wummy sloppy puppy likkle poopy den…" Crikey! I haven't heard myself use *that* voice since I exchanged private language vows with the man who used to call me Tufty Ponderosa in the brief six months before marrying me and leaving me when I was 21. But let's not go there.

I am, however, becoming a dog. It was bound to happen. You hear a lot about the perils of lack of empathy these days but very little about its opposite. Over-identification, plus poor boundary control and a need to please equals Losing Yourself, as many women understand, and I have lost myself.

At five am, when I take him out to pee, the stars are shining, the wind is riffling through the cherry tree at the end of my neighbour's garden. The moon is grinning like a loon. And I sniff the air. My ears are cocked. I stand transfixed by the waving spikes of the Cordyline and I feel a ripple of primal joy pass through my body from head to toe.

If I had a tail – and it didn't make me look like a pensioner demonstrating the meaning of the word "twerking" to a similarly aged friend – I'd wag it. I would. I also have a strong desire to piss on the lavender. Help! Inner Canine, get back in your basket, you bad bad girl.

But oh, how happy I am. This is not a mistake. This is the beginning of a big adventure. Wait… He is asleep. (Thank God!) Excuse me if I yawn and stretch and curl up on this nice floor cushion by the radiator…

Meeting And Greeting

"Socialisation" is the big buzz word in the puppy world and I am a teensy bit disappointed in Hector so far. His first encounter was with Dainius, my Lithuanian lodger. It was six o clock in the morning and I was standing in the garden in my dressing gown when Dainius came out for his first fag of the morning before going off to test ventilation systems or whatever it is he does.

Dainius is a beefy sort of bloke with a short-to-shaved haircut and piercing blue eyes. He is rather handsome in a villainous James Bond kind of way and he had not previously seen me in my dressing gown so it was all a bit awkward which possibly affected Hector because when Dainius said, "Ha! I luff dogs. Come here little doggie", and put out his own big paw towards us, Hector dashed between my legs and refused to come out.

Well, fair enough. But the same thing happened with my gentle ex-Buddhist monk friend Huw. Arriving for tea bearing Lidl's croissants, Huw immediately and properly prostrated himself on the carpet at a good distance from Hector and murmured soft Zen-ish wooing noises that even I would have found hard to resist. Hector shrank away from him like a skirt-clinging toddler.

Huw was obviously hurt because he said, "call yourself a puppy", which hurt *me*, on Hector's behalf. (*Bad* Buddhist, Hugh!)

But why the shyness? Was it the beard Huw was sporting because he was waiting to be an extra in *Far From the Madding Crowd*? The yellow baseball cap? Is Hector picking up on my own trepidation where men are concerned these days?

It has to be said that he doesn't behave in the same way with women. Sue Darling, who is well known in Bridport for her passion for puppies, came bounding scarily through the door shouting, "Come to Aunty Soooo", and then she scooped him up, flipped him over, rocked him in her arms like the Baby/Piglet in *Alice* and tickled his tummy for half an hour. I honestly think that if she had dressed him up in a christening gown he wouldn't have turned a hair. So it's all a mystery.

I think I had better try to relax about it. The trouble is that I simultaneously want Hector to like everyone I like as much as I do and – because I have been such a rotten judge of character in the past, hence the singledom – I'm also half hoping he will act as some kind of Guide Dog for the Gullible, steering me through the rapids of future human interaction with his supercanine intuition. *And*, having been ruined by boarding school, I simply cannot stand timidity or weediness of any kind. Dear me, that is an awful lot of expectations for a tiny puppy to bear.

Give him a break, Gill! Yes, I will…

Maggie

I have achieved a small triumph over my cleaner Maggie who clearly thinks she is Nanny McPhee. Maggie is a six foot Amazonian local girl of sterling character who I am surreptitiously grooming to be my carer when Dr. Alzheimer puts me on his patient list. I like her enormously and I could not do without her but she is *very* bossy.

Despite being a considerable number of years my junior she ticks me off for not watering my plants and for spoiling my kids and she won't let me choose the brand of toilet cleaner we use. Her opinions about the use of garlic are stubbornly Draculonian ("What on earth are you stewing up now!"). And last week when she went to a Burlesque show in Bournemouth, she said it reminded her of me because I fling my lingerie all over the bedroom floor.

She insisted I buy her a proper mop if I was going to introduce a dog into her regime. (Being a masochist from The North I prefer to get down on my hands and knees with a knitted string cloth). And when she arrived to meet him for the first time she breezed in, snatched the mop from Hector's jaw saying, "I'll have that, thank you! We will start as we mean to go on. Maggie's here now".

I told her I was just going to pop out to the shops and, as it was a special occasion, she was welcome to ignore her duties and play with the new member of the household if she wanted.

Well! When I returned she was out in the garden looking very sheep-ish. More accurately, she looked dogish: she had that guilty 'I might have done something you're not going to be pleased with' look that dogs do so much better than sheep. And it turned out she had allowed Hector not only to shit under my desk but to pee on the floor cushion! "You said I could play with him…" (Bad, *bad* Nanny McMaggie!)

But secretly I am delighted. The proper pecking order has been re-established around here. I am Top Dog and she is not going to get away with telling me off any more – however many conciliatory marrow bones she brings me from Rawles the butchers. Ha!

Played Out

Having entered my second childhood, I imagined that I might actually enjoy Playing with Hector. When my children were small I used to get them to play Hide and Seek so I could squat behind the sofa and read a couple of paragraphs of my book while they counted to a hundred. And I really wanted to redeem myself this time so I had been lapping up the chapter on 'Playing' in my bible, *The Perfect Puppy* by Gwen Bailey.

She suggests something to the effect of, "if you are a reserved person, see this as a chance to lose your inhibitions. Run, jump, wave your arms about. Be as silly as you like! Your puppy will soon understand that you are a fun person to be with…"

For heavens sake, I thought. Even one of my prep school reports suggested that I might try – "without sacrificing any of her gaiety" - to be a little less silly. So I was obviously born to be the good time gal of Hector's dreams.

But no. Yet another vain conceit has been demolished by reality.

In truth, the problem has not been my ability to romp around. We have a lovely time. I particularly enjoy the bit where I wedge a yoghurt pot on Hector's nose and he goes insane trying to get it off. And when I throw a ball down the garden and he comes racing back towards me and throws himself into my open arms like the final scene of *The Incredible*

Journey it fulfills every reunion fantasy I have ever had (apart from the daddy-oh-my-daddy one from *The Railway Children*).

The trouble is that after five minutes of playing I do get bored. And when I get bored, Hector, instead of behaving like a child and crying, "More! Again!", flops down with impeccable empathy and a resigned harrumph and I just know he is thinking, 'me too, mate! Bored with stuffed squirrel, bored with squeaking penguin. When's the real dead pheasant action going to happen around here?'

Last week, things reached an all time low when I found I had completely reverted to type: sitting at the dining table engrossed in my iPad and hurling things at random onto the carpet saying, "for fucks sake Hector, have this spoon".

Time, I realised, to stop this dilletantish playing at Playing and seriously up my game. And it's worked. Because I've realised something. In *The Perfect Puppy* I came across this telling line: "try not to get angry during games". Hmm. Now why would they say that? Unless Playing is not 'creative free expression' at all but actually Training, in disguise – possibly great for disinhibiting the owners but definitely designed to lay down a specific set of inhibitions in the dog.

So now I have a new *modus operandi;* bending his will to my own in a fun way and trying not to get angry when it doesn't work. "Play with this good rubber ring for dogs, Hector, and NOT with this Hobbs black suede court shoe with the snake-skin heel".

"No, Hector, we don't catch living things and shake them by the neck until they die then bury them in a nice big hole in the flower bed. We play this jolly game called Tug of War instead, OK?"

I am getting positively Joyce Grenfell about it all. And you know what? Now I view Playing as Training – something with a use and a purpose, where we are getting somewhere and achieving something – it's become a lot more...well, a lot more FUN...

Love Me Love My Dog

My 90 year old Mum thinks I might meet a nice man now I've got a dog. I'm not convinced.

Last week I bumped into Horst at the sauna. Horst The German, as opposed to Herman The German, who has long since left town to live near Seville, is my ex-lodger and he didn't want to go out with me, apparently, because I talk too much.

"I've got a dog", I said, (in the fewest words possible). And he practically knocked himself out hitting his forehead with his hand.

"I don't believe it!"

"What do you mean?"

"I have been internet dating lately and every second woman says, 'my great love is my dog'. 'My German Shepherd is the great love of my life'. They put their photos up. In the garden with the dog. In the kitchen with the dog. In bed with the blimmin' dog. I give up! The world has changed and I did not notice. Enough!"

Hmm, I thought. Now you know how we feel about the football and the cars.

I talked to Huw about it and he said, in Planet Aspergers Mars mode, "why doesn't he just put 'no dog owners' on his profile?" Very sensible,

Huw. But I – representing Venus – suggested. 'why doesn't he just go with the flow of the zeitgeist (since he is always boasting about how Enlightened he is) and simply get a dog like everybody else and his dog?'

Bridport singletons are always moaning about the lack of romantic opportunities locally and the grave compromises one has to make as a result. Some wag named this small-town syndrome 'The Bridport Pound', which, put succinctly, means: if you lived in London would you buy your shoes in Stead and Simpson?

But, as I have been told, *ad infinitum*, you meet so many people when you're out with a dog.

So get a dog, Horst. Take it for walks. You will find a regiment of eager females plodding up and down the beaches and fields of West Dorset dying to find a dog-loving partner they can whistle into one third of the bed.

As Aunty Soo said on this subject, (having successfully negotiated the terrors of a recent first date), "the thing about going for a walk together is that you don't have to look at them". In other words, you can look outwards, onwards, forwards, to a sunlit future of walking side by side through the ruts and puddles of life and always having something to talk about.

I am out there. I can give you the daily grid references if you like. Not that I'm desperate or anything. In fact, if anyone proffered a tender touch I might break into a million tiny pieces like the telephone and desk in the Skittles advert.

But think of the role-playing opportunities! I could be Elizabeth Barrett Browning, lying listlessly on the day bed with her little Flush whilst thou ministered unto me. Thou could be Byron, mourning the loss of his Newfoundland, Boatswain, who had "all the virtues of Man without his vices". I could even play the dog if thou wanted. "Woof *Woof*," as Leslie Phillips would say.

The funny thing is though, when I first met Hector, it was rather like meeting a nice new man. I was frightened. Why, I wondered? Then I realised that deep down I was assuming he would sniff out some deeply buried character flaw; that he might unearth it and present it proudly to the world from whom I had tried to hide it for a lifetime. I admit it: I was worried he wouldn't like me.

And he does! Oh Joy! He cares not a whit that I talk too much, that I am vain, pretentious, self-absorbed and greedy. Beat that, Horst. And don't say, "Ha! As long as you are carrying a bowl of minced chicken…"

Fit As A Butcher's Dog

Excuse me while I indulge in a Proustian moment. I can hear the clinking of Hector's metal name tag on his china bowl as he wolfs down his dinner and it's all coming back. My childhood. My first dog, Conker. The intense pleasure and anticipation I felt as I spooned the Pedigree Chum onto the Winalot and mashed it all together with a fork thinking, 'ooh, you're going to enjoy this so-oo much'.

I tried the Winalot. In fact, as a seven year old, I ate quite a lot of it with my sister, in the barn, pretending it was 'provisions' for our Running Away From Home game. It was very nice; nutty and wholemealy and altogether superior to the stone-baked, hand-turned 'artisan' biscuits I bought the other day from Mr. Waitrose.

The thing is, even though I have been told that dogs don't have many taste buds, I do like the idea of Hector enjoying his food. Which is why I am not feeding him Kibble. Kibble is, supposedly, 'scientifically and clinically proven' to be 'nutritionally complete'. But I'm sorry, it still seems to me to be akin to eating a diet of Cheesy Wotsits, albeit 'fortified with vitamins and minerals'. And when I think of Hector drinking water after eating it I can't help imagining it swelling up and hardening in his stomach like that styrofoam insulation stuff they squirt around pipes to stop them freezing. No!

Unfortunately, the alternative routes are making me as anxious and neurotic as the mother of a teenage girl with food issues. Am I feeding him enough? Of the right things? Too much? Well yes to the latter, apparently. Three people in the last two weeks have said he was fat. (Yes, James, YOU! And where do you think the term 'Puppy Fat' comes from, may I ask?)

He was a *bit* fat. I am meant to feed him up to 10% of his body weight a day while he is growing. And as he is on the Raw Food Diet recommended by his breeders, that is a whole kilo of meat! So, having thoroughly googled the multitude of forums on the subject, I cut his rations - hey, it's the *5:2* diet! - until I could feel his ribs again.

People go a bit stone-faced when I talk about the raw food diet though. As if I was showing off or something, attention-seeking, being poncy, faddy or implicitly criticising *their* dog -food choices. It's a bit topsy-turvy, when kibble was only invented about 40 years ago and dogs have been eating raw meat since the dawn of time.

Never mind. As with all Diets, we have already gone off the strict one we are on. I balked at the whole-mackerel, rabbit-with-the-fur-on thing in any case. And he buries the chicken wings in the garden. So I'm adding boiled rice and tinned sardines and I may even make the gluten-free liver cake recipe they handed out at dog training class. *Real* food. Yum! I think we're doing fine.

Of course, if I left him to his own devices he would probably choose those oysters of the dog world, Slugs. There are loads of them in the garden at the moment. Bright orange and ridged, like giant Haribos (Slugtastic!). And as they give dogs lungworm, I am creeping around in the dark resentfully encrusting them with my very best Maldon Sea Salt when Hector's not looking. Maybe this will make them more appetising, as well as dead. We shall see.

It's quite possible I am completely out-to-lunch. But anyway, I am off to the nice old-fashioned butchers now to buy him a nice old-fashioned BONE...

Puppy Parties

Being a puppy is not dissimilar to being retired; have a little doze, a bite to eat, another doze, a potter round the garden, scratch, yawn, sniff, sigh, drink, then flop about on the sofa watching sheep-dogs running round on Countryfile.

So Hector and I were very excited when we were invited to a party. Hooray!

It was at the vets. And it was a bit of a letdown at first. Only three dogs turned up. Rosie, a chocolate rescue Ridgeback with a bad leg, Hector, and a tiny shy Spaniel whose tail was curled so far between her legs that her back seemed permanently arched in a constipated poohing position. She was no fun at all. She ran under a chair and stayed there while Rosie and Hector dominated the floor with their wild dance moves.

The dogs had a great time. Toys. Nibbles. Bottom-sniffing. Meanwhile, we three owners sat self-consciously on chairs around the room like wall-flower parents at a school hop, staring glumly into our free tea and wishing it was time to go home.

The Spaniel's chaperone was a handsome lad in his early twenties. He was red as a plum with embarrassment, and he bore the resentful demeanour of one who has been bossed into something by his Mum. He kept blinking, frantically, as if it might help him wake from a terrible dream.

It *was* surreal. Like being at an orgy in a doctor's consulting room. From waist level upwards it was all pale green Formica cupboards, washable surfaces, kidney-shaped bowls and wall charts. And down on the floor, a Bruegelian hell of humping, hackles, bared teeth, exposed genitalia and wagging legs and tails.

In fact, the floor was so slippery it was more like a game of ice hockey. Round and round the room they careered, slipping and sliding and knocking each others legs from under them. When things got a bit rumbustious, Anna, the veterinary nurse, hurled handfuls of titbits onto the Lino and they fought each other for every morsel like poor street kids in films when some misguided philanthropist has thrown a lot of coins into the air. I had to keep lifting my knees to avoid being lacerated by competing teeth. I spilt my tea.

And over and above all this cock-tail mayhem there was Anna, bravely and loudly trying to keep a conversation going about parvovirus, fleas, ticks, jabs and pet insurance with all the grim insouciance of a seasoned hostess.

While the animals cavorted, we were encouraged to ask questions. And that was when it turned into something more like family therapy and it all looked up. I arrogantly thought I didn't have any questions. But you know when you are being brave and someone's kind to you and you break down? Well, I suddenly got a lump in my throat and it all poured out, "He barks at vases. Yes, I know! I don't know what to do. And yesterday he ate a tulip bulb. And…"

When our hour was up, the tables had turned. Hector had to drag me home with me going, "this is so-oo unfair".

But best of all, at the end, they gave us party bags! We got a yellow squeaking tennis ball, a pack of Dentu-sticks which made Hector behave like a crack addict deprived of his fix for at least an hour after eating one, a bag of promotional faux-food, a very handy handbag-sized bomb-shaped pooh-bag dispenser and, to top it all…

POULTRY-FLAVOURED TOOTHPASTE!

We went home all of a glow. I think Hector misses Rosie. I miss Anna. I think it's time we got out more. Maybe there will be a doggy dancing class in a village hall soon. We can learn the Dog Trot. Oh, I am glad the world has gone so dog doo-lally. It is hugely entertaining.

And, of course – the whole point – whenever Hector has to have his vaccs or worse, he'll think he's going to a rave. Rock On!

The Local Doggregation

For thirteen years I worked in Bridport Old Books and I spent an awful lot of that time people-watching through the big plate glass window behind the desk. After a while I could tell who was passing through the corner of my eye, by their gait, by some indefinable energy that was uniquely theirs, even if I didn't even know their names.

It wasn't a busy-body curtain-twitching thing. Just a kind of mental clocking, tracking peoples' badger-trails criss-crossing about town. There goes Mr. X who's always on his own; or the diminutive Miss Y, tripping along on tippy-toes behind her shopping cart; the old man from the Chapel in the black peaked cap who strides with such a sense of urgency and purpose.

Everyone in town is at it. Noticing. Somebody I didn't even know once said to me, "you used to wear a lot of skirts. I only ever see you dressed in trousers these days, dear". (Yes. Once I had a boyfriend…) Then there are the nicknames: Sally Cycle, to distinguish her from Sally Pilates, Sally Cookshop, Sally Ukelele. Not to mention Mad Mark, Crazy Dave, Crumpet Claire. I could go on and on.

And now I am discovering a whole new geological layer of Bridport society. Hector and I must have met a hundred dogs in the last few weeks and spotted many more about their business in the distance. It's like the time I bought a Morris Traveller and suddenly the roads seemed full of them. It's overwhelming.

People say you never ever get to know the owners' names. But as my memory has been buggered by booze, spliff, chemotherapy and age, I find I'm struggling to remember the dogs'.

There is a chap I'm often bumping into who has two attractively shaggy long-legged hounds. To me he is, 'the guy with the Jimmy Edwards handlebar moustache who wears shorts even in the winter'. But the dogs could be called Chip and Pin for all I can recall.

I won't forget the sweet punky lad with the Great Dane who called across to me, "don't worry, he won't hurt you, he was chased by a Chihuahua last week". But who *are* they? Search me.

It's getting better all the time. I've learnt that this particular dog is tired/old/lame/blind/doesn't want to play with puppies. I know that that one swallowed a fish hook and nearly died. I know that this one's owner had a hysterectomy. And I've already clocked the dogs *and* owners I would cross a river to avoid.

Since I watched the National Theatre's anniversary bash on television, I have also started noticing some striking similarities between the dogs we've met and some of our most venerably grizzled thespians. There are a lot of Gambons out there, I can tell you, and a few McKellens, Jacobis and Una Stubbsies too. It's become my latest walkies-boredom-busting game. They make a great mnemonic.

And I'm hoping all this strenuous mental exercise is forging some new neural pathways in the old brain. If not, I may be forced to take up Bridge, like Huw. God Help me! The relentless and absorbing congress of Bridport life is one of its great joys. But sometimes – just occasionally you understand -"ve vunt to be alone".

Hector Untrained

One day, working in the bookshop, I came across a copy of *The A-Z Book of Dogs* by Barbara Woodhouse. Remember her? The plummy exhortations to "Si-it!". All that no-nonsense boarding-school matron charm? Well, I'm telling you, she was BRUTAL. I was astonished.

Check this answer to a reader's question. 'Dear Barbara, my dog is very nervous and she shivers when my husband comes into the room'. Barbara: 'Nobody likes a nervous dog. Have it put down.' It was all like that! Which goes to show how fashions change. These days, social services would be called, divorce papers served, or the husband would be instructed to lie submissively on the floor and woo the timorous beastie with delicious treats.

Hector and I are starting training classes soon and, I gather, I am expected to bring a pocketful of enticing edibles to reward his good behaviour. It's the training technique *du jour*. And top of the list of suggestions is Hot Dogs (appropriately) and cheese. Well, I already tried Hot Dogs as a training treat at home and I ate the lot of them myself. Are you turning in your grave yet, Barb?

I cannot wait to start. Years ago, I used to take the children's mad dog Sox to training class. (We had to re-home the poor thing in the end. He was a Deerhound. He chased deer. Whatever was I thinking?) Anyway, there was this woman who used to come there – cashmere cardie, court shoes, pearls, immaculately saloned hair – and she used to walk around the circle, bristling with frustration, whispering to her tiny pooch under her breath in an outraged hiss, "you are a *disgrace*. An absolute *disgrace*".

It was pure Alan Bennett. Hilarious. And now I have attended our new class Introductory Evening (minus dogs) at Melplash Village Hill I can see that dog training this time round is not going to disappoint.

The village hall is painted in swimming pool blue. There are a row of blazing overhead heaters that make you feel like a pig on a spit. The doors marked Ladies and Gentlemen go nowhere of the sort. And – we are informed – the door marked Fire Exit is actually a cupboard.

Our leader, Rosemary, is of a similar breed to Barbara. She has that hefty English countrywoman build and general aplomb. Happily, she has a breezier, more forgiving approach – "we all make mistakes" – and a talent for wry one-liners. "I see a lot of dogs who think their name is Sit". "If your dog pees during class, don't worry, I shall introduce you to the bucket and the mop".

There were six of us attending and God knows what kind of an insanely conscientious swot I must have seemed to the others. I was scribbling away in my notebook the whole time. It was just too good to miss.

There was a slideshow. It went something like this: "All puppies bite. They have a set of teeth. Next. The next slide please, Judith, that's right dear, the button on the left. We need to teach them manners… yes, dear, that's the one. She doesn't know how to do it. Why do people buy dogs? Next please, Judith. Oh, she's getting the hang of it now. Well done dear. I have a one command policy with dogs, just say things once, I do not want you turning into one of those dreadful owners who say 'stay… stay…STAY' all the time. I think she's got it…"

We have seven more sessions to come – with dogs – and this includes a trip to a farm with cows and sheep. Rosemary says she can instantly spot an animal that's going to be a nuisance. I think I need a pocket Rosemary to take on dates.

The only thing that's been bothering me is this: why, after 19 years, do I only recall the cashmere cardie lady (see above) and not a single other participant or incident from that particular portion of the past?

Yesterday, preceded by that sickening lurch of the stomach that indicates the coming into consciousness of a great truth, I realised. The answer my friends, potentially, *c'est moi*!

I do hope Rosemary is going to train me up. Until then, "Out, out, out, dark shadow collar-yanking lady. OUT…"

Breaking Bed

I am slipping. No, I have slipped. The starting-as-I-mean-to-go-on has stopped. Hector is sleeping on my bed.

It happened slowly, like an addiction, like starting smoking again when you have given up. It crept up on me, in incremental steps, each one accompanied by thorough rationalisations.

I have always been very bad at sticking to my guns. Once, years ago, I happened to be sleeping underneath a grand piano (don't ask) with a friend who wanted me to get underneath his blanket (so to speak). "No, no, no, no, oh all right then", I went. Same with parenting. "You want a Macdonalds? No, no, no, thrice no, ok, all right then". Hopeless. This time I wasn't even begged!

He was doing fine in his crate in the porch. I'd put him out for a last pee. I'd say, "into your bed, Hector", in a bright, cheery, comforting voice, and that was that.

Then one night there was a lot of thumping in the street at 2am. It sounded like someone using a defibrillator. It was the gas men, digging. Oh, poor Hector must be scared, I thought, he must be wondering what on earth is happening. He's probably cold as well, and maybe lonely. Surely this qualifies as Exceptional Circumstances? Just this once?

Then we went down to my Mum's. His crate is in my room. I could hear him, all night, scuffling and yawning, pointedly. The crate is only three feet from my bed. So what's the difference? "All right, Hector, just this once".

Then I was invited to a party. Would I rather be woken at 6am, hungover, and have to spend half an hour, before I've even had a cup of coffee, calming a dog who is (as usual) delirious with joy after a night apart? Or have him on the bed, opening one sleepy eye at 8am to check I am still there?

Four weeks on we're sleeping together twice a week (and I have bought a dark grey duvet cover). Not every night because, with a clever dog, you only have to do something once and he thinks, "Right, Boss, got it. That's the plan". And he's not allowed under the covers, you understand.

Now, after six years of enjoying the deep peace of the double bed alone, it's Deja Vu time. I am waking up at four in the morning needing a pee and finding myself trapped under a long and heavy hairy leg. I carefully lift his foot. I slowly slither sideways onto the floor. ""Ssh", I say, "go back to sleep. It's all right. Everything is all right."

And it is all right. Apart from the guilt. In fact it's bloomin' luvverly. I can hear him breathing. I can feel his dear heart beating. My legs are warm as toast. So what if he is "just a dog" as even Huw is sometimes moved to say. I've missed this.

I used to read all that stuff about old people and pets and I'd think, 'that's nice but what's it got to do with me?' And here I am. Old. With a pet. With perfect blood pressure and a steady pulse and, without even trying, taking long, slow, yoga-ry breaths as all my tension drifts away. Ah! It works. It's true.

So I'm doing it for my health.

But that's a half-truth. So, like Walter White at the end of Breaking Bad, I'll say it out loud: I am doing this for MEEE. Because it is convenient. But most of all, because it makes me feel ALIVE...

Sons And Puppies

I am becalmed in the Bermuda Triangle between Christmas, New Year's Eve and getting-back-to-normal. The winds are wuthering outside the window. The rain is slashing down. It is 9.30 in the morning and still dark. And we are NOT going out for a walkies in it. It's a Holiday, right?

Frailty – thy name is Woman in the festive season. My brain feels as if it has been wrapped in puff pastry and baked. And I am behaving like the Dianne Wiest character in *Parenthood*, wringing my hands, looking pained yet cravenly hopeful, cringing with maternal and dogternal guilt, and creeping round like Mrs Overall, with trays.

It's like 101 Dalmatians around here. Huge pale spotty human puppies with litters of their friends. They don't turn out the lights at night, they leave wet towels and chewed-looking shoes all over the floor. They sniff out hidden delicatessen specialities. It seems they have blocked the toilet. And, of course, they are all still asleep, piled on top of each other, heaving with hangovers and worrying smokers coughs.

On many occasions, since having Hector, I have reflected on the joys of being completely without responsibility for another living being, the chief one being the lack of guilt. Nothing I did or failed to do in those glorious few years of solitude screwed anyone else but me. As soon as I got Hector the guilt kicked in again, that horrible feeling of not ever getting anything quite right that dogged the parent/partner years.

Yesterday, I woke up dreaming I was being assertive with the children. "Joe. I have asked you ten times to put your rucksack and your presents and your trainers in your own room and you say "later, Mum" and now it's ten times 'later' and I'm telling you, if all this clutter which is driving me insane is not moved right this instant it is going in the garden, in the rain, and Hector will probably pee on it."

What happens? I tidy up all morning single-handedly and then I creep upstairs at 2pm trilling, "anything you want, darling?"

"Breakfast", comes the duvet muffled answer.

"What would you like?"

"What is there?"

"Eggs"

"What kind of eggs?" and so on. And off I shuffle to the kitchen calling, "chilli sauce with that?"

I love it really but poor Hector has been demoted to the status of baby brother. He has been enthusiastically voted a great addition to the family but the boys either wind him up into a frenzy rolling around on the floor and playing tug of war just before bedtime, or he is excluded from their more sophisticated games. "Mu-um! Hector's eaten the Monopoly money. He can't come in. Get off me, Hector. Stop it. Ouch. Fuck off. Mum!"

And if Hector could talk he'd most likely be saying, "Mu-um, the boys won't let me play, the boys are being mean to me, the boys won't give me any of their sweets".

Last night, there were about 15 young people living it up in the living room and Hector was sitting right outside the door, pathetically scratching at it with one paw. I happened to observe this heart-breaking tableaux because I shut myself out too, banished myself to the landing with Netflix and a bottle of *Framboise Eau de Vie* I stole from my Mum with a view to marinading strawberries in the summer (when will I learn?) and a roll-up I stole from the kids.

As they say, if you pride yourself on being a good Buddhist spend three days with your family. So, lovely as it all has been, I've had enough of the holidays. And on that note I shall wish you all a Happy New Year and get on with scraping burnt turkey pilaff off the wok.

Oh damn. It's stopped raining. Walkies anyone? Hell no. Later. I am going to have another naughty roll-up and a glass of guilt and start-as-I-mean-to-go-on again tomorrow.

Counting The Ways I Love Thee

The boys call Hector "Mum's new boyfriend". Leaving aside the grosser implications of this kind of teasing, and without getting soppy about it, it is true. I love him. And it's no different from loving a human being, albeit a mute with some disgusting habits to which I am immune.

Firstly, the phase of idealisation is firmly in place. I think Hector is a genius. When Mozart is played on Radio 3 he goes completely still, absorbed, transported. He can also tell the difference between rain water and tap water, (and eschews the chlorinated, fluorided latter). Brilliant! Not to mention totally attuned to topical eco-consciousness. I ring my Mum every day to report his latest achievements. I bore my friends. And although I *can* see through my rose-tinted varifocals, I still believe he is far more intelligent and beautiful than anyone else's dog.

I have fallen in love with men because of the way their hair curled behind their ear, with the way their fingers looked on a fret-board, with a single muscle in a nice brown forearm. And the way Hector's tail has this dear little swirly bit on the tip of it – well, I could moon over it all day.

Then there's the way, when he runs in front of me, his back legs sort of swerve to the left, like a car in a high wind with unbalanced air pressure in its tyres. Sweet! And when he is trotting along failing to balance a four foot long stick in his mouth, it is as poignant and heart-stopping as watching your six year old stutter his only line in a school play.

I have also slipped into a worrying old love habit of asking, "Are you all right? What do you want? What are you thinking?" a hundred times a day.

Which all begs the questions: will I, in time, find that the sight of his swirly tail-end fills me with unaccountable annoyance, not to mention fury? When he performs his latest trick, will I start thinking, 'Hmm. You really think you're something, don't you?' I cannot believe I will. So. Maybe this time, Lady Happy, maybe this time, tra-la-la.

Unfortunately, the purity of our love is already being compromised by popular training methods. When puppies nip, they say, you should cry out "ouch!" in a wounded tone whilst dramatically rubbing your sore hand and pretending to cry. This does work. Hector is most gratifyingly disconcerted and attentive when I do it. But isn't it a bit like 'turning on the waterworks'? A tad manipulative?

They also say that if your dog does something you do not like you should turn your back on them, walk away, refuse to stroke them, with-hold treats, and generally, says Rosemary, "use your body language to show them who is boss". In other words: SULK.

Well, I have been to Relate and Couples Counselling in all but one of my 'relayshunships' so I'm not sure if these tactics are quite kosher. Should I try using the "I" word as opposed to the accusatory "You"? Here goes.

"Hector. I feel, if you don't mind my saying so, that I would be much happier if you...I'll start again. Please don't be offended, Hector, but I feel – and I know it is *my* problem – that although I fully appreciate that it is your peculiar – or should I say distinctive – way of demonstrating your love for me, I would prefer it if you simply licked me rather than sitting on my head".

Does this work, despite the awkward archness of relate-speak? No. of course it doesn't. Get real, Gill. "Hector, fuck off with your smelly ass". Better, no? And surely more like the intimacy I have been told I am afraid of.

At least I talk to him. I chunter on all day long in that affection- ate chivvying way you can observe in happily married couples who no longer expect to be listened to. "Honestly, Hector! For Heaven's sake! What *am* I going to do with you? ...I think perhaps we should have a nice piece of steak for our supper, don't you? Well, of course you do, you greedy old mutt". Etc

But who else is around to insult without offending. That's love for you. And love ain't no walk in the park – even if you are with a dog.

Doing The London Walk

The Metropolis! Ye Olde Stamping Ground. Yes, imagine me in my black Ralph Lauren/Waldemar Hospice coat, my furry black Russian/ Mencap hat, my handsomely accessorising black dog. How cool am I? Not! Hector behaved like a complete country bumpkin. I now have rope-lead burns on my left hand. And my black suede boots are ruined because I forgot there was mud in town too and didn't want to sartorially compromise myself with unsophisticated Wellingtons.

London is like a Disneyland for dogs. I wound down the windows as soon as we hit Hammersmith and Hector's nose went into overdrive, like Samantha in *Bewitched* on speed. Imagine: drains, trains, skunk, spunk, fast food, incense, multi-ethnic blood and vomit, a veritable Northern Lights of olfactory explosion.

Not to mention pigeons, en masse, milling about insouciantly and re- fusing to be chased like the rooks by the River Asker. And drifts of tasty ketchup soaked KFC wrappers in the gutters; and tempting fox shit to roll in all over the garden where we stay.

I lived in London for 24 years and, in a way, nothing much has changed. On Hampstead Heath people are still trying to jog and talk about Freud in the same breath. And good old Kentish Town is still full of people with mental health issues, talking to themselves. But – maybe it's just me slowing down – London seems to have speeded up. It's like those films of city nights with whizzing arcs of coloured lights blurring to a frantic jazzy soundtrack. The whole time we were there Hector was like, "Where's the fire? Where's the party? Wait for meee…" as zillions of people sped past on all sides. Hence the infuriating failure of all the "Heel" training I have achieved so far and the resulting rope burns from restraining him.

I used to have a dog in London. I inherited him from a boyfriend. He was called Chen The Wonder Dog and he was so street-wise that he used to get all four feet on the road and then, with impressive bum-hovering precision, drop a steaming turd right on the edge of the pavement thus cleverly managing to obey the letter rather than the spirit of the Camden by-laws.

I used to let him out in the morning and he would roam for a couple of hours and then come home, announcing his return with a single "Woof" on the doorstep. I used to cycle all the way to Putney with him galloping along beside me stopping at every red traffic light. When I think of it now it is as shocking as seeing the Michael Gambon character in *The Singing Detective* smoking in an NHS hospital bed. Chen was practically the only dog on the block and poop bags were unheard of.

And now there are so many dogs! Not just appropriately small box-room-flat sized dogs but Wolfhounds the size of horses and every variation of the fashionable spoodle/cockadoodle/shi'ttypoo/hoodlumdoodle, all dashing around Parliament Hill off the lead. Mayhem!

I got so tense that one time, traversing a zebra crossing with gritted teeth and assuming that Hector was only pulling on the lead behind me because he was gawking like a tourist again, I was alerted by a fellow passer-by with drawling sarcasm saying, "he is *trying* to have a pee". The shame! I could just imagine her at a dinner party, "there was this dreadful woman, dragging this poor little puppy along by the neck…"

This time I brought his crate to London so I could have left him and gone off to an art gallery or something. But I just didn't have the energy for it. And, for once, I am unreservedly glad to be back to the wellies and the straw-chewing and all the other Ooh-Erring business my London friends think I do down here.

Tomorrow, we are going on a Farm Visit to Symondsbury with Hector's training class. He will learn to 'Walk-On By' a lot of horses, cows and sheep. After the London Experience it's going to be a doddle, even if he does eat the cow-pats.

The Dog's Dinner

Lunch actually. With nine humans and three dogs. How civilised. What a joy to be able to take Hector to a regular social occasion. But was it the dogs who lowered the tone or the drink?

Rex – not a dog despite such a doggy name and often called Bryan in any case – has bought an ex-social club in Weymouth complete with crowbarred fag machines, sticky carpets and vile maroon banquettes. It is already half-gutted so the dogs had what resembled a huge dark multi-storey car-park to be social in.

Hector, Rhubarb and Colin – a terrier despite his droll human name – had a great time skating on the slimy green algae-covered outdoor roof terrace. And, as they played, we did our human thing, talking about iniquitous mini-roundabouts and traffic calming schemes and other pressing matters until Hector was sick, "someone" peed on the floor, the drink kicked in and the tone inevitably descended.

Nico was doing his Sunday Skype with his parents in New York by this point and we hoped they couldn't hear us. We had got onto The Closet, a new gay club in Weymouth. It was a short step from there to *Embarrassing Bodies* and then, as happens these days, people came rolling out of the closet as secret Daily Mail readers, fattists and lots of other 'ists', and by the time the delicious homemade syrup sponge arrived the conversation has turned irreversibly scatalogical.

It was a good thing half the company were dog owners because who else could so enjoy hearing about the time Rhubarb ate so much frozen sheep shit that she sicked up a pile "bigger than her head" all over the gear stick of Rex/Bryan's van.

Someone said that cow-pats, (Hector's favourite canapoo), provide 'good flora' for a dog's gut and I owned up to giving Hector Yeo Organic Natural Yoghurt for this purpose. Such hilarity! "How middle class!". And from there on it was all pooh talk and worse. (How *upper* class!)

The dogs eventually played themselves out, calmed down and slept. And we all became more and more raucously 'off the lead', running out to do our roll-up bonding rituals by the door and wolfing down the cheese and Rex's homemade apricot pickle.

It was lovely. But I did think, next morning, when I woke up worrying, as usual, 'did I talk too much? Did anybody notice how greedy I was with the cheese straws and the garlic bread?', that even with age and confidence, with the relaxed and happy company of friends, there's always a residue of social anxiety. (Did Colin's owners, Ross and Radhika, who I had not met before, think Hector was a bully?). And dogs don't have that.

Dogs are sociable creatures, just like us. But it seems so effortless. Hector will flatten himself, even into a puddle, a hundred yards from some oncoming dogs and, with others, he will stand his ground, instinctively negotiating every subtle position on the sub/dom spectrum. But does he agonise? Does he worry about whether to give one sloppy nibble on the muzzle or the full European two-sider? I am sure he doesn't. And I don't suppose he thought twice about whether Colin minded being straddled under a bench.

Mind you, I have been to parties with Rex/Bryan where nobody would have minded being straddled anywhere at all. But that was the drink, yer honour. And that's the point. We drink to get as levelled and chilled and 'in the moment' as dogs. We agonise next morning about whether we behaved like dogs. And the dogs are probably better at socialising than us in the first place, and without a drink!

Thanks to being sick – I think it was excitement and the whole apple I gave him in the car on the way to keep him quiet for a minute and a half – Hector was not sick down Jane's neck on the journey home, as she graciously pointed out. Saved, mercifully, from another embarrassment to fret about.

Sometimes I wish I was a dog. But perhaps some people think I am one. Oh no! Pass the brandy, Bernard...

Be Here-ish Now

When I first got my iPhone I went a bit mad with the apps, as you do, and installed one called Meditation Bells and another one called Insight Timer. The idea was they dinged – or dang – at random intervals throughout the day to remind me to Stop, Look, Listen, Breathe and hang out in The Now. I kept forgetting to set them.

Now – hooray, delete, delete – I do not need them. Hector does the trick instead.

I have been meditating for 20 years and recently I graduated myself to the 'every moment of my life is a meditation' level which, apart from being irritating to other people (Ho Ho), is obviously a self-serving delusional rationalisation enabling release from the frankly boring business of sitting still for 45 minutes every day. Of course, as a practised meditator, I have learnt to recognise and accept such frailties without judging myself. And then I let them go. Poof! Done. But I still need to be re-minded and Hector leads the way.

Often I will be busying about in my usual speed-of-light way when I will notice Hector suddenly stop whatever he is doing and freeze. He seems to be listening intently; to a footfall in our alleyway, perhaps, a distant bird, or, if I were to be fanciful, to the angelic harmonics of the universe, inaudible to human ears. Anyway, he is, in these moments, Attention personified. So I stop and listen too.

When we go out, his uncomplicated enjoyment of everything he encounters, his absolute 'hereness', is infectious. I begin to relax into my stride, my shoulders drop, I take deep breaths, consciously feeling every muscle working. And soon the dull mist of banal mental list-making and bothersome tax returns clears to reveal the morning, the satisfying shape of Bothen Hill, the various shades of the sunrise, (and, this morning, Celia, in mismatched wellies on the wrong feet!) Result!

Dogs, they say, live in the moment all the time. And given the zeitgeisty fashion for Mindfulness these days it may explain why dogs and all things doggy are gathering momentum in the media by the minute. I bet if I started looking on the internet I would un-earth some weird conspiracy theorist type nerd who thinks that aliens are planting more and more dogs in our midst to teach us lessons in compassion, forgiveness, presence and what have you, in preparation for the coming of the Age of Aquarius or something. I will not be a bit surprised if Ekhart Tolle produces 'A Little Book of Dogs' by the end of the year.

I have to say, I am not *entirely* convinced that Hector does live in the present. For a start, he spends at least two hours of every day in an anticipatory fever for the future; that is, half an hour before walkies twice a day when he appears with a lead in his mouth, and half an hour before mealtimes when he sits by the kitchen door wagging his tail hopefully. Not very Zen, if I may say so, Heccy.

Leaving that quibble aside though, The Zeitgeist certainly moves in mysterious ways. I never imagined when I got Hector that I was part of some mass cultural Dogs R Us moment. But it is becoming clear that I am. And it is surprisingly comforting too, now that I am old and alone, to see that I am not, after all, An Individual, as I hoped when I was young, but, happily, swooping about like a starling in formation with a lot of other people of my ilk or generation.

And if people believe that dogs have something to teach us, apart from being loyal foot-warmers, I am happy to go along with it. God knows, every guru I ever fancied following has turned out to be clay-footed if not an out-and-out abuser. I might as well follow a muddy dog. Hector has taught me how to put something before myself again. And not before time. Ding! Saved by the bell!

I'm an old dog on the rough road, with a puppy on the path to some kind of enlightenment, I hope.

To Do Or Not To Do

That is the question. And the jury is still out. My Dad once said, testily, that I was swayed by the last person I talked to, by the last book I read, and rarely has that been more true than now. I think I have decided. But then again, I haven't.

When I asked Hector's breeder if I should have him 'done' he winced. "Oh, no, please don't", he said. Well, it is his profession to breed beautiful black Labradors who might go on to sire more beautiful black Labradors. And he is a beautiful young black man so of course he's going to say that, I thought.

Then I asked Jane. "Oh yes", she said, "do it. He will love you so much more". He will, she added, love food more as well. It is hard to imagine how Hector could love me and food more than he does already. But, it swayed me all the same.

So I have been standing outside Good News, my local newsagent and old-fashioned general corner shop to canvass local opinion. Good News was recently 'done' and it became a horrible chain 'convenience store' which, with routine Bridport genius, is now dubbed Bad News. And opinion has been equally polarised.

I have talked to people who did their dogs and regretted it, and people who didn't do their dogs and regretted it, and one who gave me a long angry lecture on my social responsibility not to litter the world with any more poor rescue dogs needing homes. (What? Not even progeny with such illustrious ancestry? Go away!)

Google, as usual, was no help. Every opinion under the sun. "They", for instance, say that dogs who have been done don't get testicular cancer. This is like saying that you won't get a brain tumour if we cut your head off. Very helpful.

I asked our venerable trainer, Rosemary. Her advice, unsurprisingly, was the most balanced. Don't do it, she said, unless they start humping all your visitors, cocking their legs on the furniture, attacking other dogs or otherwise displaying 'behavioural issues'. OK, I thought, I'll wait and see.

But my neighbour Erica, whose two dogs, Stig and Tug, are on the lively side if not completely mental, says she did them and it hasn't made the slightest difference.

It is also beginning to feel like a moral dilemma. The only reasons I can find to do it are selfish. It would be 'convenient' not to have him roaming far and wide frothing over *les femmes*. And it would be heavenly to be loved even more (without being mounted).

But the reasons not to do it are also selfish. And they include not giving any satisfaction and vindication to those ex-lovers who already think I am a selfish and castrating bitch.

To be fair to them, I have already started to say to Hector, even if only in jest, "you'd better be a good boy or it's going to be the snip for you, miladdio." Old habits die hard.

So, what's my gut reaction? What is in my heart? I look at Hector, so big now, so masculine and virile, so beautifully lithe and boyishly lively and I just cannot bear the thought of doing it to him. But when has my gut or my heart ever led me into anything but trouble?

I have approximately six more months to deliberate. In the meantime, Hector's balls are hanging in the balance and I shall have to try to grow some. Hamlet, you didn't know you were born, boy...

Achilles Heel

I hate, I absolutely hate heel-training Hector. Everything else has been a doddle: Wait, Leave, Sit, Fetch, Drop, Stay, This Is My Break-fast Not Yours So Go And Lie Down In Your Bed. I say it, he does it. (Well, you know, after I have said it three of four times.) But "heel" is my weakness, my downfall as a credible trainer of my dog. Every day is Groundhog Day; back to square one at the start of every walk.

I've got to get it sorted. Hector already weighs 20 kilos. He is very, very strong. If he were to take off after something with me on the end of the lead I would not be able to restrain him. Picture the final flourishes of Torvill and Dean's Bolero performed by Hector and I skating past you on a slick of wet leaf-mould on a pavement through the middle of town and you will see how imperative it is that he learns to submit to this simple (ha!) command. (Especially since I have been boasting about how well we are doing.)

'Heel' is a stupid command though. It is impossible to say with any authority. It is, in a word, lame. Why not 'back' or something with a nice hard consonant attack? I am sick of saying it, over and over, "heel, HEEL, Hee-Yull". Sometimes I just growl – "Grrrr". He knows what that means. And the other day I found myself involuntarily doing this furious little flamenco tantrum stamp (accompanied by a growl) and he backed into position like a terrified courtier.

That's the worst of it really, the reappearance of this Red Queeny side of my character. I thought I had vanquished her when I banished the last bloke and the children fled into their own lives. But here she is again, alive and kicking up. She has this appalling tone of voice, an unconsciously crafted blend of impatience, frustration, disappointment and sheer menace. And her vocabulary becomes more florid and pompous with every step. "Hector. I categorically will not tolerate this abominable behaviour for one more instant." That kind of thing. I blame it all on my expensive boarding school education. I was raised by Head-Mistresses. Sometimes I become one.

Hector smells the tension in me too, and consequently will do anything to get away from me. In other words, when I am at the end of my tether, he runs to the end of his. So it's entirely counterproductive; like screaming "go to sleep!" at the top of your voice to your babies. Stupid. And shameful too.

There is one effective technique I have been using. It feels a bit like being in a car that's being towed, but, instead, when Hector pulls and the lead goes taut I let it slow me down until I stop completely. When it slackens off again we walk on. This is really very satisfying in a mildly sadistic way. "Ah, you get the message now, eh? You pull, I stop. Simple. Got it? Going NOWHERE if you pull".

The main drawback of this start/stop approach is that it makes me look as if I'm suffering from some neurological disorder with a symptomatic jerking tic. (The Woman Who Mistook Her Dog For A Husband, perhaps?) I am getting strange looks. Of course, if I have a handful of *food* Hector will walk to heel even when he isn't on the lead. But I'll have to wean him off food bribery eventually. And, according to Rosemary, the way to do this is to smear your hand with meat paste. Bonkers. Do I really want to be spotted in Bridport behaving like a broken mechanical toy and smelling like a 1950's picnic lunch? No, I don't.

So, the upshot is that I'm walking him on the lead less and less. This is much more fun for both of us, but it is, once again, counterproductive in the wider scheme of things.

In the wider scheme, Hector is perfectly trained to behave perfectly in public. I obviously have a profound investment in this because otherwise I would not be getting my knickers in such a twist about it. And, as I have only recently managed to restrain the worst of my own wilder impulses, I am assuming that this is linked to my current need to project an ideal of punishing restraint onto him. Don't ask me why. My own psychology becomes more puzzling to me the older I get.

At least I now understand something else that has been puzzling me; which is why I never see any of the many dog-owners I know walking in town with their dogs. They've got frustrated with the 'heel' thing just as I have. I'm guessing this because I do glimpse them flitting through the woods during the ungodly hours when few are around to scrutinise their training achievements. I wish we could join them more often.

Unfortunately, as I have been perfectly trained (hobbled) myself, I feel duty bound to plod, plod, plod on persevering until we get this right. If you pass me on the street in the next six months you will no doubt hear me hectoring: "One day, when you can demonstrate to me that you have truly understood the meaning of the word 'heel', then, and only then, my boy, will we be going for more walkies on the wild side".

Naturally, I am not letting Hector know how fervently I, too, look forward to that day.

Reverting To Type

On our morning walkies we keep passing a guy who once sold me a dangerously dodgy car. I have been blanking him for so many years that when I first saw him on the doggy path, I thought, with curiously twisted logic, that he wouldn't recognise me. I probably would have continued to ignore him but for the fact that he also has a black Labrador. So now I say "Good morning" and sometimes even, "river's very swollen, isn't it".

Coincidentally, the only other person I have ever blanked in Bridport or anywhere else is also on that doggy path and I have started to say good morning to her too. Dog ownership is making me positively Pollyannarish. But being nicer to people I dislike is not helping in my search for dog-related people I can write about without worrying if it is going to piss them off.

The reason I am thinking along these lines is that Huw says I could put more characters in my Dogalogue. When I started out, my Mum enquired -somewhat disingenuously, I thought – if I asked peoples' permission before writing about them.

I managed to fudge a defensive answer, ("well I hope they'll be flattered!") whilst privately thinking, "I am a journalist, Mother. Am I going to go, 'Oh, Mr.Dictator, would you mind terribly if I wrote about your torture chamber?' No."

It is tricky all the same. I could write volumes about the characters in this town – if I was fearless and ruthless and imminently moving to a different country. As it is, applying the six degrees of separation theory, I have, in the space of three paragraphs, potentially offended the loyalties of about fifty people and I haven't even mentioned any names.

Which is why I have been trying to think in terms of 'types' instead. There's *The Outsider*, for example. This person (OK. Man) has a rescue cur with a name like Kafka. He is a misfit; wounded, haunted, hard-done-by, probably a frustrated artist with very low self-esteem which is why he has bought a best friend even needier and more woebegone than himself. His dog is thin, grey and shivery, with eyes like a child in an NSPCC advert. He (man) has a van, and seeks out places with a lot of bracken where he can contemplate injustice in the world (and personal slights) while Kafka (Karma, Castro, Cohen) makes up for lost time running in the wild.

And I've pretty much made him up, of course, from a combination of one of my many alter egos, elements of the kind of wastrel I am at-tracted to/repelled by, plus a little bit of objective observation; by which means I hope I have created someone who is both recognisable and unidentifiable at the same time. I am exhausted. (No wonder I never finished that novel!)

So, back to reality. There is one old lady on the doggy path who is both a character and a type. Her dog is very ugly and aggressive. When he snarls at Hector she says, "Ah! Look! They really like each other don't they." When he snatches at my pockets with his yellowing fangs, she says, "Ah! He knows you've got a little treat for him in there". And I'm not a bit bothered that she will be alerted to this portrait because she is so lost in her dotty, sentimental and deluded adoration of her hound that she would not recognise herself or him.

She could be me, of course, in another few years. (Except for the fact that Hector is beautiful and not in the least aggressive). I have heard that same warmly indulgent 'what's a girl to do?' tone in my voice when Hector has planted his great muddy paws on someone's newly dry-cleaned trousers. "Sorree, he is just a puppy".

Oh well. There we have it. There is really only one type of dog owner; the type who cannot credit the fact that nobody likes their dog as much as they do.

Can I go back to writing about myself now, please? Because, you understand, it's not just narcissistic. It is self-protective too.

Ms Dolittle

As a teenager, before I grew a critical faculty, I was unashamedly seduced by that old ham, Anthony Newley, talking to the animals in *Dr.
Dolittle*. I now know that any Irishman whispering anything in my ear
could get the animal in me to do anything at all, at all, at all. But 'dat's
buoy de buoy, me little darlins' (Stop it, Gill!), the point is that it's not
what you say it's the way that you say it.

When we had our old dog Chen we used to amuse ourselves saying
"good boy" in a "bad boy" voice and then the reverse, which probably
made a knitted dishcloth of his neural pathways, but it proved the point.
He'd roll over on his back in ecstasy as we rubbed his tummy, crooning,
"you're a naughty boy, Chen" in a loving and caressing tone.

It's got to the point with Hector that I hardly use real words at all. For
instance, he has this deviant habit of immediately taking over my spot
on the sofa whenever I get up to make a cup of tea. I used to make a big
Goldilocks type play of it when I got back. "Excuse *me*! Is someone sitting in my place?" Now, all I have to do is put my hands on my hips and
utter one of my expanding repertoire of noises and he shuffles along.

Body language obviously plays a big part. In fact, the art of dog-speak
requires an operatically exaggerated level of vocal and physical performance. At the moment I am teaching Hector to catch things in mid-air.
It's a kind of keep-him-happy-during-Coronation-Street thing. And I

behave like a one-woman football crowd. When he catches the ball I jump up out of my seat, I punch the air, I shout yay, whoop, and wave my arms about. And if he drops it I can do that huge collective wail of disappointment too. Words, schmurds, who needs 'em?

There is the universal language of disgust as well. "Uggh!", "Blear-ghh!" and "Arrgh!" are particularly useful for either expressing dismay at something he has already done or warning him off doing something in the first place.

Not to mention "Grretonowdavit", for really extreme situations. This 'word' was invented by my father (yours too?) when my sisters and I used to be so bold as to knock on the bathroom door when he was in there. It is a sound that seems to emanate from the very bowels of the earth. And it's effective meaning – "Scarper. Now. Or else you're for it" – does no justice to its primal power as an utterance.

But Hector is way ahead of me in this game. In the mornings I take a cafetiere and my iPad back to bed to read the papers online. After about half an hour, Hector always does this massive noisy "have you *forgotten* walkies" yawn. And I like to play along; "Hmm. I wonder what the time is? Could it be… no… is it? Yes, I think it is the time for wa…"

What I had not realised is that prior to this performance I, apparently, draw in a long preparatory oratorical breath. I know it now because, yesterday, I began to inhale and he was off the bed, down the stairs and sitting by the back door before I could even say, "Hmm". Talk about finishing my sentences for me! We are practically the same being.

And whereas even a month ago I might have used partially intelli-gible sentences like, "what are you up to now, you silly doggit", now I find myself just going, "waddawaddawaddawadda". It's become a ful-ly-fledged private language, a seamless incantatory riff of endearment and expletive and I hardly draw breath all day long.

I think I should be studied by a feminist linguistic theorist. For 85% of every day, I am alone (except for Hector). This means that I am free;

from observation, convention, polite social self-editing and a great deal more inhibitory nonsense. And I really don't believe that I have regressed into an infantile pre-verbal babbling gaga-dom. I think I have advanced; into a post-verbally expressive state of flowing female purity and bliss.

OK. It's been a long hard winter. I *might* be going just a tiny bit stir-crazy. But Hector knows what I am on about. Don't you, Hector, you snuffleooffleawfuloffalus...

Our Daily Dread

Hector's not a free dog: he has a number. Well, I imagine it's a number, something like MWXv85@2zzzzz. And it has been sewn under his skin, apparently, etched on a grain of rice. Surely they must have meant, 'something the size of a grain of rice'? Whatever. I may not want this image etched on even the smallest grain of my imagination but I'm very glad that Hector has been micro-chipped because I'm very frightened of losing him.

I did lose Chen. Once he wandered off on Hampstead Heath and found his own way back to Paddington on a freezing snowy winters night. But then one day he didn't make it home. I rang every police station in London. I put posters up on lamp-posts. I went to look for him in Battersea Dogs' Home every Sunday for three months. It was one of the worst things that ever happened to me. And if you are allergic to black humour, skip the next paragraph.

We think that Chen was made into a coat. There were gangs, we found out, coming down from Manchester with vans to steal good-looking dogs. 'Korean Wolf-skin' coats were appearing, coincidentally, on the stalls of Northern street markets. And what made it so darkly ironic was that one of the little step-sons always used to say, "when Chen dies I want him made into a pyjama case so I can have him on my pillow all day long". It was not to be.

Last Saturday, on our market, I bumped into Simon who also has a puppy called Hector (Grrrh!) and we commiserated about the terrible fears we had for our dogs. Simon reckons he is suffering from some kind of Munchausen-by-Proxy Syndrome, projecting his own hypochondria onto his Hector, rushing off to the vets with the slightest worrying symptom.

We had a real "Ooh, I *know*" conversation. Alabama Foot Rot! God yes, terrifying! Toxic palm oil on the beach! Electronic cigarette cartridges containing fatal doses of nicotine!

I am so scared something is going to happen to Hector that the only time I risked tying him up outside a shop I had to keep going back to the end of the queue – the only place I could see through the window to check up on him – which rather defeated the object so I put down my basket and left without my shopping.

I told Simon that as a child, I liked to make myself cry by thinking about my poor dog's demise. I still do it. I imagine myself like a human Greyfriars Bobby, moping about the house disconsolately, bursting into racking sobs when I come across his chewed up Squirelly beneath a chair.

Someone said to me recently, about living alone with a pet, "it's good to have another heart-beat in the house". What a beautiful way of putting it. But another beating heart is another heart that could *stop* beating, in a heart-beat… Oh dear, I am welling up again.

This is Pre-emptive Grief Syndrome, apparently. (Yes, it's a Syndrome! I'm not just a self-indulgently morbid freak.) But does it work? It didn't with Chen. I still grieve 29 years on. And anyway, what if the tables are turned? And I go first?

This is the kind of thing that occupies me during attacks of 5am Nameless Dread Syndrome. It adds a poignant twist to my perennial having-a-stroke fantasy; in the ambulance, with a shaking finger, I spell out 'H.E.C.T.O.R?' on the palm of the handsome paramedic's hand. Or else I croak, pathetically, "my dog…who will take care of my dog?"

I've worked it out though. Employing The Daily Mail method of risk assessment, I am guessing that I am a hundred times more likely to die of being a human being than Hector is to die of being a dog. Does that make sense? No, of course not. Nothing makes sense. And the only thing that is going to put an end to Fear of Death Syndrome is jolly old Death himself. Whoopee!

But guess what? The other day we missed it by a whisker. I forgot to latch Hector's crate when I nipped across the road to Bad News for the local paper. Screeching of brakes and horns. Hector, in the middle of the road. Irate woman at the wheel of a car. Mad horrified dash back across the road by Culpable Me. More screeching of brakes.

And now I am feeling preternaturally calm. I may, in fact, be *paralysed* with fear.

Anyway, we are both grounded. Life is a bitch. Death is a dog. And I have decided: if we are both inevitably going to go, we might as well do it pleasantly, together. "Butcher. Two of your largest finest T-bone steaks, please…"

Teen Spirit

When I was on the cusp of adolescence I had a rare row with my Mum. My then dog Conker had dug up the onions or something. I was defending him. The heated 'words' that were exchanged included "come here", and I ran off. I headed for the open fields. She chased me. Oh, the sheer exhilaration of realising that I could outrun her, that she couldn't catch me.

So, it is with a wistful sense of identification that I stand, these days, blowing impotently on my Acme whistle while Hector bounds off into the distance with a newly defiant fuck-you spring in his step. At nearly seven months old Hector is officially a teenager.

Luckily, since he's not political or idealistic or full of oestrogen, he will not be flying out of the dining room in tears, shouting, "anyone who owns a house with more than two bedrooms is OBSCENE", as I did.

Luckily, since he is not a 21st century boy-child, I will not have to watch him in front of the mirror poking at a non-existent midriff, wailing, "Look! I *am* fat, Mum". Or hold his friend's heads while they vomit fruity smelling alco-pops into the flowerpots. Or fight a losing battle over Thank-you letters. Or…

So, what have we got to look forward to? "Adolescence is a selfish time", the puppy manual says, and "you will feel like a failure". "It will seem as though he has forgotten everything you have taught him" and "what you want will be much less important to him".

Yup! It has begun. We have had one unaccustomed pissing indoors incident. We have a new but ongoing table-chewing situation. In the evenings he is literally bouncing off the walls, careering round and round the living room like a cage-motorcyclist in a fairground. If I didn't know better I'd think he had chewed up a month's supply of Berocca.

He has developed Attitude too. When I call him, he dawdles in a brazenly 'I'll come when I'm ready' kind of way. I swear, sometimes he's laughing at me. (Maybe that is the disconcerting effect of the new mountain range of scary white pointy teeth). And these days, even when I'm proffering two cupped handfuls of FOOD, it's clear that every leaf, post, stick and bottom is a great deal more interesting than me.

It's a funny feeling; sort of vaguely wounded but irritated too. I used to feel much the same way when I had cooked a vast vat of pasta and the kids just whistled through one door and out the other like a through-draught, shouting "not hungry" or "eating at Matt's" and I'd be left standing there, forlornly holding up the serving spoon like a conductor in front of an empty orchestra pit.

How long is it going to last? Six months at least, the books say. But the old ladies on the path just laugh at that and tell me, "wait until he's eighteen months and he's got the muscle power as well". And some say five or even seven years, which, if true, will mean that, like me, he will segue from an extended adolescence straight into retirement.

At least when this stage is over he will remain at my fireside, chewing my pipe and eating my slippers, and not jetting off to countries where they decapitate people, or The Future, with barely a backward glance.

In the meantime, Spring has sprung – Hooray! Perhaps that's all that has got into him. I must say, I am feeling ready for a bit of digging up the garden too. And what is that I hear? Ah yes, it's the song of the other mud-crusted dog-warblers trilling, "Come here, come here now, come here now or else I'll..." Somehow I think this promises to be an energetic summer...

Anthropopwhadyamacallit

'Anthropomorphism' is a very difficult word to pronounce, so I hope nobody tackles me on the subject after the cocktail hour. Or anytime at all really, because people get very heated on the subject. When your dog has polished off a stolen six-pack of eggs and he's slinking around refusing to meet your eye and you say, "Ah! He knows he's been a naughty boy", they will yell at you.

These Anthropodeniers – and yes, it is a word – don't credit animals with any inner life at all. "He's not feeling *guilty*," they cry, getting redder and redder in the face, "Guilt and shame are 'higher complex emotions'. He is simply frightened of being punished. It's a learned response from the last time you went ape-shit". etc etc.

Well, OK, I get what they are saying. It's very easy to ascribe emotions to our dogs that they probably don't have. I was wondering, only today, whether Hector was bored, when it occurred to me that probably he doesn't get bored (like me) at all. He's more like a laptop that has gone into standby/screensaver mode; with a kind of instinctual pragmatism he goes to 'sleep' until booted up into instant bright alertness by a word like 'walkies' or the sound of a fridge door being opened.

But if I *imagine* he is bored, I'm going to take him out and throw him a stick. If I *imagine* he is lonely, stuck in his crate while I am at a party,

I am going to make my excuses and leave. So my anthropomorphism, even if it is 'bad science' or sentimentalism, is also a kind of empathy and it works in Hector's favour.

Sometimes I watch Hector twitching and yelping in his sleep and of course I speculate about the fields of his dreams and the creatures he might be chasing or fighting there. Who wouldn't? You'd have to be practically inhuman *not* to project your human-ness onto your animal.

There are limits, of course. A friend of a friend has a Pug and they go to Pug parties, apparently, where the dogs are bibbed and tuckered up as cheeky Bellhops, Nurses, *Petit Matelots*. So far, thank goodness, I have resisted such loopiness.

Which is not to say I haven't been tempted. I wanted to get Hector in a Pork Pie hat .(I didn't mention the word out loud in case he got his Pavlovian hopes up.) I couldn't find one. And when I see black Labs with red paisley neckerchiefs I always think "nice!" – until the inevitable associations impinge. ie. men with a taste for single malts, with garages full of vintage cars, with ancient Nortons that they want to take you on the back of... No-oo!

I suppose, the truth is, I feel a little guilty about it all. (She says – exercising her often regrettable capacity for 'higher complex emotion'.) Week after week, putting thoughts into Hector's mind, and words into his mouth, turning him into a 'character', roping him into the vacated roles of partners, dead or gone, and children, scattered. I do feel as if I am sinning, somehow, against the purity and integrity of his animal essence.

In my defence, I blame my pedigree. I have been bred on a diet of Winnie the Pooh, Wind in the Willows, Beatrix Potter, Mickey Mouse and Animal Farm.

And Hector is still a mystery to me. ("What's your horoscope, Hector?", "Hey, I'm a Labrador, I'm biddable, affectionate and loyal.")

That's why I'm guided, ultimately, by his tail. Upbeat, down-beat, no-beat, drooping, wagging, round and around like a Catherine Wheel when he meets a favourite doggy friend or Huw. Does that mean he is happy as we know it? Or simply animally excited?

"Are you happy, Hector?"

"Woof"

"What does that mean?"

"It means that, as your Dad used to say when he was losing an argument, 'it's semantics, just semantics…'"

"OK. In that case, shall we bury this bone of contention and head down to the beach?"

"Woof woof"

"Sorted"

Duvet Days

Hector and I are unwell. We are languishing. And it is at times like these that I find myself envying middle class Victorian women who, for all the oppressions they had to bear, did have the culturally sanctioned option of 'taking to their beds', where they were allowed to lie, for decades at a time, sipping cups of beef tea with no more precise a diagnosis than 'nervous prostration'.

That's what I have got. I have been nervously prostrated by a bit of Everything; it's a seasonal transitiony thing, a fear of impending mammogram thing, a 'what's it all about Alfie' thing, not to mention writing these essays which often feels like standing in the dark on the cliff-edge of the universe lobbing all my spinning plates Greek-restaurant-style into a big black hole – minus the satisfying and cathartic smash at the bottom.

I have also had a sort-of intimate proposal, gently suggested and graciously (I hope) declined, which has nevertheless opened gaping fissures in the foundations of Peace Of Mind Towers in East Street. A wild hoolie of suppressed emotion is now whistling through the cracks. Wizened old demons are scratching underneath the floorboards, flapping round the light-bulbs, blundering into windowpanes. If it wasn't for Series Three of *Nurse Jackie* and Fish Fingers (can I really manage ten?) I don't know where I would be.

As for Hector. On Sunday we went for a long walk at Hinkhams Farm with Pete and Marion and their large Dalmatian puppy Lily. Two Grannies and a Grandpa ploughing across the churned earth of the Marshwood Vale with two powerful, seemingly inexhaustible Canine Retirement Enhancers, locked together in play-fight combat, barrelling around the field and felling us, one after the other, with whoomfing blows to the backs of the knees. "Bloody dogs!" we grumbled.

Anyway, Hector must also have eaten about three pounds of various kinds of animal excrement. Literally full of shit, or (help) worse, he lay listlessly all evening in his crate, coughing, retching, gagging, snuffling, snorting and occasionally throwing up. Sometimes he dragged himself up the stairs and slipped around my legs like a cat before laying his heavy head in my lap. Every half hour I dragged myself downstairs and crawled waist-deep into the mouth of his dog-cave to commiserate. We were just not ourselves.

Of course I googled it. Asking Google questions is therapeutic in its own right. It is like sending a little S.O.S in Morse code; 'Dog.sick.call. vet?'; 'white yellow frothy vomit?'; 'Symptoms bloat?'. And before you know it, reassured, you're back down to 'How to make Kale crisps?' and 'When to plant Aubretia?'.

But that was Sunday night and on Monday there was no change. I boiled some plain white rice, dragged Hector to the river to eat some grass, took some Vitamin D3 and an Epsom Salt bath, and we took to our beds again.

On Tuesday the only thing I really absolutely had to do was to empty the compost bucket. I didn't even manage that. 'Will the world end if, for once, I put potato peelings in the general rubbish bag?' Fuck it!

Then, on Tuesday night, when Hector was snoring so loudly that I got up to google 'something obstructing dog's airways?', this appalling thought just pinged into my mind like an email alert: if something happens to Hector you won't have to write The Dogalogue this week…

Gill Capper, what are you *like?*

Well, I'll tell you what I'm like. When I saw, the other day, that a man had been taken to hospital with head injuries because he was hit, in the high winds, by an NHS sign that read, 'Are You Feeling Under The Weather?', I laughed like a drain.

You see? We need a break. It is Thursday and time to 'gather'. Hector is better. ("Get *Off,* Hector!") I am better-ish. And so Hector and I are googling 'Spa Holidays Pets Welcome?' And we may be some time…

On The Road Again

I am currently on day twenty-four of the super re-energising trendy Nothing-Nice diet (no alcohol, cigarettes, caffeine, chocolate, meat, fish, dairy, sex or added sugar). Hector has put on about three kilos and he's learnt to bark and swim. We are as fresh as daisies again and hot to trot.

Which is a good thing because, frankly, I was running out of things to write about. My Mum got away with saying it out loud: "do you think it's because…perhaps…you know… the novelty of Hector might have worn off a bit?" What? No! But yes. But no, it's just that at the beginning he was a bit of a Project. And for the first six months he changed, he blossomed, daily. And now…well, he's just a dog. Adored. But. He eats. He sleeps…

Someone suggested, oddly, that I could "throw him in the river". That was before he learnt to swim. But even so, 'dog thrown in river so owner could write about it' may indeed resemble the kind of non-story that shivers our timbers down here in the land of The Bridport News but it's not exactly going to excite anyone except the RSPCA, is it?

So, the upshot is, I've bought an ancient motorhome and we're going on the road. It's going to be *Travels With Hector*. And it came about because, in the last few weeks, I've done a lot of Visiting and I have not experienced so much guest-paranoia or anxious creeping about since the time I went to my best friend Janey's 18th birthday party and was caught by her mother (Lady Hayter Hames of Chagford, Devon), naked, drunk, disorientated and on all fours, traversing the pitch-black landing of her stately pile trying to find the door of the room in which she'd prophylactically billeted my boyfriend.

Visiting, plus a dog, is the best possible way to experience the heroic politeness and hypocrisy of ones friends. When Hector tramples all over the flowerbeds, jumps on the sofa, shakes puddle-mud all over the fresh laundry, eats the cat food and generally causes mayhem, our dear hosts, one and all, persist in saying, "don't worry about it! Really. It's fine. I wish I had that energy! I was going to have that sofa re-upholstered anyway", albeit, I notice, with an increasing lack of conviction and the occasionally leaked deep sigh.

As the culpable guest I twist myself into agonies of apology and self-deprecation: "he'll calm down in a minute, honestly, he's just so pleased to see you. And he's still a puppy. I would leave him in the car but it's a bit hot, no? And he might feel abandoned. Yes, I know, don't say it, I am one neurotic doggy-mama! What have I done? Don't answer! Is there somewhere I can stow this enormous bag of bones, ha ha?" It's very stressful.

Even at Mum's where he is one of the family and allowed on the sofa it isn't much easier. Mum doesn't sleep well and Hector's very early morning routine of peeing and breakfast is a logistical nightmare involving three flights of stairs, a balcony and a self-slamming pantry door. Years of eavesdropping have endowed me with precise knowledge of every creaking floorboard in the house but try teaching that to a beast with four feet and clicky toenails. I might be the only dog owner in England trying to get her dog to obey the command, "Tiptoe, for fucks sake!"

So, as you can imagine, I have been feeling a little despondent about the summer. What shall we do? Where shall we go? Why am I feeling ever so slightly sick? Oh yes, I know. It's because for the two years prior to getting Hector in which I successfully talked myself out of getting him, I used to say, "this is the first time in thirty years I have been free. Why the hell would I want to tie myself down with a bloody dog?" And now I've gorn and done it.

Well, we've got the Romahome now and we're off to explore Wales in a couple of weeks. Just him and me. Yes, free. And if I hadn't been watching *Hinterland* I might be looking forward to it more than I am, what with all those spooky reservoirs, bleak quarries, black water, brooding men and murderers and mountains… what am I thinking? Don't answer…

Luckily Hector is immune to such nervous flights of fancy. He is, as always, a constant source of inspiration and courage. And he can bark. So, let's hope the whole adventure gives us something to write home about.

And not: 'Pensioner, 61, with suspiciously hoarse Labrador, found crying in the back of a 1992 Citroen surrounded by sheep'.

Procrastinations

Margery Romahome – who used to be called Margaret (after Thatcher), then Marguerita because she belonged to a Chilean, and now Margery after Mum, Nana, and the old lady I used to read to – is a Wendy house on wheels and Hector and I have had hours of fun playing in her already. She is full of little cubby-holes and there are two high, deep, shelf compartments which run from end to end. Yes, one side for Hector and one for me, whoopee!

In his bit Hector now has: tripe sticks, bone-shaped biccy treats, three brand new tennis balls, ball-hurler, Furminator, retracting lead and choking lead and gypsy rope lead, Squirelly (who now smells like an armpit), wet wipes, flea comb, poo bags, tick remover, portable water-bottle/bowl, and a few tins of sardines in case of a no-fresh-meat emergency. (Very Enid Blyton!)

In mine: scissors, matches, notebook, biros, torch, umbrella, radio, binoculars, tea-lights, tea-light holders, reading glasses, Iphone charger, Marmite, First Aid, bunting, loo roll and a trowel for morning business in the woods. Truly, I can think of few satisfactions in life that come close to this kind of nest building activity.

But, predictably, the perfection of the moment of complete preparedness is immediately corrupted by reality. First off, three or four times this last week I've had the impulse to give Hector a biccy treat or a game of ball only to remember that all his equipment is in Margery who is parked three streets away.

And then … well, we haven't actually slept in her yet. We have experimented with Making A Cup of Tea, but only in the car-park. And even that did not go smoothly. The gas turned out to be On when I thought it was Off so when I turned it to what I thought was On it was Off and I had to flirt with the man from Central Motors and give him money for a pint to conduct humiliating -"ooh, I'm such a *girl*" - investigations.

I tried to dog-proof the upholstery too. The seats, fore and aft, are covered in vile beige-brown chintzy swirls like armchairs in a tired old people's home. I covered the back ones in green velvet curtains from the loft and, on the passenger seat, I draped a red, suitably retro looking tartan rug which I tried and failed to anchor with the prongs of the headrest. Everything slipped to the floor as soon as Hector jumped in. Soon there were muddy, re-sale-deal-breaking paw prints everywhere and, at that stage, all we'd done was to go to Lewesden and Langdon Hill for a couple of bluebell walks.

Our first proper driving excursion was to Mum's to show off Margery and to confirm my role as 'completely bonkers' in the sibling hierarchy. It was a very retro driving experience. Unlocking the doors feels like opening a cash box. There is no central locking and no power steering and you have to count to 15 before turning the ignition in order to warm up the engine. But we got going at last and were soon tootling happily along at 50mph listening to Van Morrison cassettes from the dark ages, with Hector nobly riding shot-gun beside me. Yee-Har!

Unfortunately, the passenger seat proved too small for Hector to lie down on, even when he curled himself into the shape of a Danish Pastry. He climbed into the back and reclined, regally, like Cleopatra, on the banquettes, sometimes right behind me with his head resting on the top of mine which was very heart-warming but it must have looked, to oncoming traffic, as if I was wearing a strange Davy Crocketty road-kill hat.

And, as Hector tried out every possible lounging position in the back, by the time we reached Exeter, the cushions had eased their way down into the central foot-well thus obscuring the window in the back door that makes parking possible. Of course, this also obscured the terrifyingly visible tail-gatery of all the drivers angrily crawling up the hills at 20mph behind me, so that was a bonus. But I was pretty much of a nervous wreck by the time we arrived.

We still haven't slept in her. And yesterday I received an email from PhileasDogg.com's Jane who has published a book of dog-welcoming hotels and B and B's, many of which provide special dog throws for the chairs and beds, and complementary bowls of haggis on arrival, and menus of charming dog-walks in the regions and all manner of other dog-centred delights. I simply cannot bear to work out how many nights I could have afforded in these luxurious establishments for the money I spent on Margery.

We still haven't slept in her. And the comforts of home and my lovely bed grow more desirable by the day; the local walks where I know I can let Hector off the lead; the rivers Brit and Asker, two minutes from my door, with their easy places to get in and out; the glorious finery of a Dorset May … I just don't want to go away.

But go we must, if only to spite those friends who have laughed with a decidedly dark edge to their affection at my "enthusiasms". Who knows, maybe the trip will finally teach me the lesson of contentment with the things I already have.

First, however, I still need to play with heating and the water-pump, the fridge, the hook-up cable and the Porta-Potti…

A Fanny Festival

When I bought Margery Romahome I naively imagined that Hector and I would now be able to go to lots of lovely festivals. But no. Dogs, it seems, are rarely allowed. Apparently they used to be tolerated at Glastonbury but then they started roaming in packs at night, barking, fighting and scavenging, followed by hoards of stumbling cider-heads calling, "Scrumpy! Come 'ere ya bastard..." and that had to be that.

So it did seem magically serendipitous when a Facebook message alerted me to Fanny's Meadow Festival in Martock where dogs-on-leads were welcome. On Friday, at noon, we cruised into a setting fit for a Midsummer Night's Dream; the River Parrett winding lazily through field upon field of buttercups and purple clover, past the little clumps of face-painted faery children, to the sound of whistling kettles and Borage-blue-eyed young men making plangent music on tin drums. 'Twas ever thus. And happily there were lots of us oldies, the inventors of such gatherings, comparing the comforts of their ingenious van conversions and suffering from stove-and-awning-envy.

We settled in. Within three hours of arriving I had eaten my entire weekend's ration of chocolate and Halva and looked at my watch a hundred times. Hector, dutifully on-the-lead, had been attacked by four aggressive off-the-lead dogs who seemed to belong to the crusty techies busy with the PA and drinking too much river-coloured home-brewed beer to notice. But it was a glorious evening. Hector swam, and I forgave him for swiping three rashers of crispy bacon from right under my nose.

Predictably, however, we woke on Saturday to pouring rain that lasted for the next 24 hours. I attempted to practice a Zen-like equanimity, with the mantra, "It is only water. Mud is only earth…" but the duvet got so damp we were forced to abandon books and bonios for frequent forays to the main arenas.

On one of these expeditions Hector and I found ourselves in the Henry's Beard food tent, sitting on a tiny square of sodden coconut matting, comforting ourselves with a large slice of cake whilst listening to an acoustic duo fronted by a chubby girl in striped Alice-in-Wonderland tights and denim shorts singing a song with the lyric, "I want to live but I must die…"

It was then we noticed, attached to a woman wearing what looked like a 1950's swim-cap with large pink rubber flowers around the rim, there was a fashionable Poodle-spoodle-doodle in a tight-fitting bright pink waterproof four-legged onesie with a zip up the backside and a hole for her tail. How we laughed! But the whole ensemble was so grossly incongruous (in a split-crotch-panty kind of way) that I persuaded Hector (forcefully, with a hand over his eyes) that she was not his type and we progressed across the flattened plain for an Indian Head Massage.

Well. In the evening, we were just in the middle of sharing a delicious chilli with home-grown broad beans provided by my camp neighbours, Clive and Jane, and peacefully listening to the Niagra splash of Clive periodically relieving the awning of its watery load, when we heard a loud insistent barking.

On and on it went. We decided to investigate. And what did we find? Only the Poodle, locked in a dark shed, tethered to a pallet, without a bowl of food or water, looking as miserable and shame-faced as you would expect an abandoned dog to look when its owner had obviously gone to so much trouble and expense to make it win the best dressed dog-in-the-manger award.

Most of the gathering clan around our camp fire balked at actively interfering, but Jane, who clearly has Somerset Warrior genes, had no such qualms and off she marched through the waist high wet cow parsley saying, "I am going to liberate that dog". Having done so, off she strode to the main tent where she ferretted out its owner who was getting trashed at the front of the stage and tore her off a dozen strips.

"I told her, 'you're not fit to own a dog'", reported Jane triumphantly. To which the owner apparently retorted, lamely, (but possibly in the only way one can retort to a patently just accusation), "well that is your opinion". "Can you believe it?" Jane said, "she's a yoga teacher too!" Ho! Way to go with your spirituality, boho-yoga-chic-lite-fashion-victim!

But it was nice not to be the one in trouble with the dog. That very morn I had been ticking myself off for using Hector as a child substitute, (worrying if he was going to be grumpy all day after an unusually late night bopping in a tent). But maybe, after all, it is a good thing. At least I made sure he was sleeping before creeping out for the frantic Klezmerish antics of The Destroyers on the final night.

I didn't stay long. I preferred it in my van, all cosy with a nightcap, Hector, and the music I am used to on my Iphone.

We left on Sunday morning for a blessed shower and a non-composting inside bog. But thank you, Pan, for giving me the hippie bug again because clearly the gods *were* smiling on us; first a doggy-friendly festival on our doorstep, then an exciting schadenfreuden-laden dog-themed drama to report. I think it is a sign; we're on the right path for us this summer. West Wales, here we come. And next time I will pack more chocolate.

A Dog's Days In Wales

Our camping trips seem to be falling into a bit of a pattern. The first day is glorious. (This is The Life!). The second day it pours (What am I doing?). The third day I have almost had enough but the potential shame of giving up so early drives me through days three and four and on five we are home-sweet-home feeling valiant and relieved. Well, me that is. Hector would have a whole different story to tell.

Camping, for humans, is perverse. I have realised that I enjoy it chiefly because the most banal of routine domestic tasks become imbued with a revitalised significance directly in proportion to the difficulty of achieving them. Cleaning one's teeth in a field with a plastic mug of river water, for example; "Oh, I'm so resourceful and free-spirited, look at me spitting on the mossy stones and wiping my mouth with the sleeve of my PJ's, I really must learn the names of all these birds when I get home", and bingo, I am having a this-is-the-life moment.

Dogs, being generally un-jaded, do not have to force themselves through such ridiculous hoops. For Hector, every moment of his life is a this-is-the-life moment. Which means that he is the perfect travelling companion. Whatever we did last week – sleeping overnight in a beach car-park and being woken at 6am by a Farmer's Market being constructed all around us in a storm, for instance – Hector's attitude was, "Oh! This is what is happening now, is it? OK. Fine with me".

For Hector, of course, five days in Wales meant a welcome upgrade from the two shortish walks a day plus umpteen hours watching my eyes travelling across the iPad. Four rivers, three beaches, one estuary, two large gardens, six small towns, a boathouse, meadows, forests, pubs, two new doggy friends, (Bilbo and Mattie), and a load of unaccustomed treats. In a caff in New Quay he was allowed a whole rasher of back bacon and half a sausage left on the next table, and at The Ship in Llan-grannog, lamb-shank fat and six new potatoes. I actually heard a small boy saying, "Daddy, that dog is *too* happy".

I was happy too. Wales, I discovered, is not full of people who hate the English and speak in Welsh just to annoy you. It is very pretty, very friendly, with less traffic, and reassuringly, just like in the south-west, every village seems to have a Blues/Cajun/Appalachian music festival with wonderful locally-tailored band names like Bronwen Shag.

And as I collect eavesdroppings like other people collect shells, Hec-tor's silent non-yattering companionship was just the ticket. My favou-rite of the holiday was a publican telling a customer that there were no Fish Specials on the chalk-board because, "our fisherman is also the lo-cal policeman and he's on nights, see?" Closely followed by the General Stores proprietor who, when asked if there were any newspapers left, replied enigmatically, "All gone. It's that kind of a day, isn't it".

But the absolute highlight of the holiday was a very noisy one. For a couple of nights we stayed with Christa and Roger who Rose and I met in Spain last year. And thereby hangs a tale. They were dog-sitting in Spain for a friend. And when we all went out for a meal the two dogs followed our car. Hours later, we spotted them sitting patiently by the town boundary sign, and even though it was dark they recognised the car, got up, wagged their tails and loped behind us all the way back home. I was so impressed and moved that it was then, I think, that the desire to get a dog of my own began to crystallise.

Anyway, Christa and Roger live in the deep dark woods by a river, (with a yurt for hire on Airbnb) with Mattie and Bilbo who, being very old, suffer from an apparently vet-recognised condition called Random Barking. Christa, Roger and I, being quite old, had our own form of random barking ie .late night drunken acapella singing in the back of their Transit, Isabel, after closing time in Llangrannog, when we howled practically the entire *oevre* of The Beatles, in harmony.

Back at their house, two nights later, Roger lit the sauna by the river. And as we sweated, we continued baying; all ten verses of 'There's a hole in my bucket, dear Lisa' and many more old favourites whilst Hector waited patiently outside to join us in our periodic dashes, naked and shrieking, into the cold brown rushing waters. I don't know quite who barked the most but as I said to Hector, "this is SERIOUSLY The Life!", to which he might have replied "I told you", it was that magical.

On our final night we camped at the Penpont estate near Brecon (maze, walled garden, orchard, dovecote, rhododendrons, firepits, wicker sculptures, swimming hole by the River Usk). Hector and I were the only ones there. Why? The others had listened to the weather report.

The next morning there was a terrific pre-dawn thunderstorm that had Hector bouncing off Margery's walls as if he'd been flipped around the inside of a pinball machine. And such torrential rain! I couldn't even get out for a pee. So that was that. Without even making coffee (unheard of) I stowed things away, drove off, with my Wellingtons (it turned out) on the wrong feet, and didn't stop until we'd crossed The Severn Bridge.

We were back in Bridport by ten am. And when that same evening (sunny), sitting outside The Tiger, Hector was offered a whole packet of pork scratchings by a dog-soppy drunken youth, I declined on Hector's behalf and told him, "We are not on holiday now, you know..."

The thing is, since we've been back, Hector seems to expect more from a day than I had previously led him to believe was possible. He stands and stares at me. "What? What?", I cry. But I know. We're obviously going to have to do all this again…

Going Swimmingly

You heard it here first: swimming with dogs is the new Swimming With Dolphins. Well, you know what it's like these days. People go swimming or running or whatever, as they have done for millenia, and suddenly it's Wild Swimming and Wild Running and there are books and websites and hundreds of people converging on secret beauty spots and ruining everything.

Not that Hector gives a toss. There were twenty dogs sploshing around in Hampstead Ponds last time we went to London and Hector picked up an ear infection that cost me fifty quids in anti-biotic ear drops from the vets but I'm sure he thought it was worth it.

For months, when he was younger, all he dared to do was paddle, but he soon got into his stride and the first time I noticed that he was actually swimming it brought a lump to my throat. I was so proud of him, I was like a parent at a sports day; "Come on, Hector, you can do it", as he struggled across The Asker with a jumbo-sized log in his mouth.

Doggy-paddle is such an effort-full and inefficient stroke that any man or beast who's doing it looks as if they are swimming for their lives against a strong tide, whether they are or not. And there is something so touchingly earnest and determined about a swimming dog.

Hector, with his long head and his sleek wet slick-back hair, looks like a seal when he is swimming. Breathing through his nose he makes this soft puff-puffing sound. When his feet find a solid bank again he wags his tail, sweeping it across the surface of the water, slapping at it like a newly landed fish. And when he shakes the water off it's like a Mexican wave rippling through his body from head to tail, leaving him sprightly with joy. I could watch him doing it all day.

'Watch' being the operative word until this week. Due to climate, temperature and time of year, I have been reluctantly confined to the banks and shores in a stick-throwing capacity.

There is quite an art to stick-throwing. A stick that is too short, thin, or light will not go far enough. It will also fail to make enough of an alerting splash so Hector ends up dipping his head under the water cormorant-style or swimming in circles looking for it, frantic and inconsolable, like someone who has failed to save a drowning child. If it is too long or fat or heavy, however, there's the risk of clonking him on the head with it as he follows its trajectory towards the expected point of entry.

A two stick policy is also essential if you are to avoid your dog dancing tauntingly around you while you shout at him; "for Christ's sakes, how can I throw the bloody stick for you if you won't drop it first, you stupid animal?" (It is at times like these that I question my fond assumptions about Hector's intellectual genius).

I was warned off swimming with him. "No!", people said, "he will lacerate your bare flesh with his claws". But for the last week we have been swimming every morning at Eype beach and we have only had one minor Incident. I was swimming with Rose, and as she was basking on her back with the toes of her Crocks pointing skywards, Hector (understandably) mistook her footwear for two of those indestructible rubber dog-toys, Kongs, and I had to emit a loud "Jaws!" cry to save her feet from being Retrieved.

But generally, in the sea, Hector has turned out to be the perfect gentledog. With the extra buoyancy of salt, there is no need for furious paddling and he glides serenely up and down the bay, weaving circles and figures of eight around me, keeping a respectful distance.

This morning there was no-one else around. The sea was very still. The sky a cornflower blue. No sound except the wheeling birds and nothing but dear Hector's head between me and the far horizon. Puff puff puff, we went…

So. You can forget the toy boys, face-lifts, trekking in Nepal: swimming with dogs is my *Rejuve de Jour*. I feel like a nine year old again. If the summer continues like this I may get back to three, two, one. And then what? Puff. I will disappear completely, merged, at one with the primordial soup – or 'The Drink' as my father used to call it…

Hang on! I think I have hit upon some great new insight into my addictive personality. Crikey! Yes, I remember; as a child I used to want to drink the whole sea. It was like a painfully intense thirst… for Everything. A kind of homesick feeling for the future.

Well, well. This is something to meditate upon as I'm crawling out towards the shores of my second childhood. How glad I am that Hector is doggy-paddling along.

After Glastonbury

Hector is almost fully grown so I suppose it is time to 'let go', so to speak. I thought I had let Joe go when he went to his first Glastonbury, aged sixteen, but I didn't manage an entirely clean break. I was very jealous – because I had run away from boarding school to attend the first ever Glastonbury myself – and I kept ringing him on his mobile asking irritating questions like "have you seen Leonard Cohen yet?" ("Duh! Who?")

Seven years on, Joe is taller, hairier, a graduate, and, it has to be said, he has lost the golden peachy bloom of his youth. He likes Leonard Cohen now. And after Glastonbury this year, he not only thought it appropriate to discuss with me, in academic detail, "the illegal substance choices of my generation" but he also thanked me for washing his sleeping bag AND he volunteered to take Hector for a walk.

But do I trust him with Hector? Not quite. I fussed. "Now. Take some bikkies in case you need to bribe him to come, and use the poo bags, it is anti-social not to, and don't let him off the lead near the road or let him pull because I am still training him and…" I even texted him anxiously two hours later to say, "usually feed H at 4.30 so don't be too late back".

My fears were well-founded because Joe is obviously not completely grown up yet. Firstly, when I called him, he thought it was a hoot to tell me that Hector had run off the edge of the cliff. Then, when Hector presumably began to cramp his style on the beach, he called me; "Mu-um. Can you come and pick Hector up? My friends have just arrived and…" Yes? Hector is requiring you to put him before yourself? And now, when I am in the middle of preparing dinner, you want me to negotiate the inch-wide lanes to Eype, in my unwieldy Romahome, at a time when everybody else is coming the other way? How about, "put your feet up, Mother, and I'll bring you a takeaway".

But how grown up am I? My own generation wanted to die before we got old and now we are refusing to grow old before we die. And that is why, I suppose, I am rattling around the country in a campervan still hoping that something really exciting is going to happen to me, and with all the same longings that I felt as a teenage girl walking towards a row of 'yobbos' sitting on a wall.

Four days after the end of Glastonbury festival, Hector and I were, coincidentally, in Glastonbury town itself. Glastonbury has not grown up at all. Every single shop is still called something like 'The Magyk Cauldron of Light'. And when my circus clown friend Robert and I walked Hector up The Tor, we met a musician called Dragon, a purveyor of Celtic Space Folk, who gave us a Breton tune on his mandolin and told us, with ecstatic optimism, about an imminent shift in conscious-ness in The Universe. Not before time, I'd say.

Anyway, we were going to a gig. The very word 'gig' echoes down the years since 1968 in my Father's Lady Bracknell tones, repeating, "going to a 'gig'?", as if I had invented the word. And now I rather empathise with his bewilderment.

Robert's son's reggae band were playing in a pub. The music was so monotonous that I soon found myself in the back yard where I was offered a joint by a raddled woman of my own age called Hawthorne.

When I wove back into the black hole of the back room, I sat down next to a bearded young man, with the white naked torso of a shop mannequin tucked under one arm, who asked me if I knew anyone whose demons were getting the better of them. "Yes," I said. "Me. What on earth am I doing here?"

On reflection, I realise that the honest answer to my own question is that somewhere below conscious intent I actually imagined I might Meet Someone. Honestly! Grow up, Gill!

As for Hector, he is growing up at seven times the annual rate that I am. He is already slowing down and showing signs of a more mature attitude to the sound of the doorbell, the sight of moving sheep and the temptations of cow-shit. I must admit that part of me wants him to be an old dog who doesn't need so much exercise, who is, perhaps, even a little crippled, happy to lie on the sofa being couch-potatoey with me.

The morning after the gig in Glastonbury we went to a caff for breakfast. (We'd had a rough night in the Avalon Campsite which is owned by a bitter and officious blonde who used to run a fairground and who locked the main gate at 10.45pm, giving me, fortuitously, an excuse to leave the pub before the end). And I was delighted to notice that the menu offered The Executive Breakfast: 'Coffee, fag and an aspirin. £15. You exec types can afford it'. As the retro-hippie in the queue before me said as he was handed his own breakfast (an enormous slice of retro-Victoria Sponge), "Hey! Legenderry!"

But reader, I chose the healthy option. Then, before we left for home, in my capacity as a responsible dog owner, I put Hector before my profound distaste for climbing hills and took him for another run up The Tor. We chased around and around the summit like Ian McMerlin whipping up a vortex for a spell. Now, how grown up was that?

Bad Hair Days

The word 'grooming' has acquired increasingly distasteful overtones of late but my own distaste for the word goes further back, to a time when being 'well-groomed' was practically the highest compliment that could be paid to a woman and not one I particularly wanted paid to me. My Dad tried to get me to be well-groomed with a mixture of bullying and flattery; "you've got a bloody good pair of pins, I don't know why you don't want to show them off" and so on. I didn't wear lipstick till I was forty and then, with perverse poetic justice, I fell in love with a man who wanted me trussed up in pencil skirts and seamed stockings every days of the week.

Little wonder, then, that when the puppy nurse began her little lecture on Grooming, my eyes glazed over and I had to suppress the impulse to hum a loud crazed tune with my fingers in my ears. Clean Hector's teeth? I don't think so. (Chewing bones will surely see to that). Clipping toenails? (He is not a lap dog!) Cleaning out his ears once a week? (Are you kidding?) The only concession I made to grooming was the tender ritual of wiping sleepy-dust and grass seeds out of the corners of his eyes, and a quick run of a brush through his coat when I remembered. A lick and a promise, as they used to say.

The other thing - and how laughable it seems now – is that I was so besotted with puppy Hector that when he didn't moult for the first few months, I persuaded myself, egotistically, that I had lucked out with an extra special, unique, one-off, no-shedding Labrador. Ha!

For months now there has been hair, hair, everywhere. There's a permanent slick of it, like the line of crushed black seaweed you sometimes get along the beach, along the carpet underneath the edges of the sofas and the armchairs. It silts up corners, floats like dust-motes in the air. I find it in my dinner, in my mouth, my trousers, on my toothbrush, stuck to walls, top-dressing all the skirting boards, woven like a kind of scratchy tweed into every piece of soft furnishing material in the house, and even on the highest tread of the spiral staircase up which Hector has never ever trod. "How did it get there?" is my constant refrain. It is without a doubt the worst thing about having a dog, and, like the pain of childbirth, people do not warn you.

I bought a Furminator. 'Brush for ten to twenty minutes', said the instructions. Ten to twenty minutes! Even two minutes made my shoulder seize up. And it tore at Hector's flesh like a combine harvester. I was harvesting at least half a carrier bag a Day. The very sight of its vicious little teeth made him cower like Bill Sykes's cur. And still the hair kept coming.

So now I've given up and given in. What the hell! Hector swims most days so at least it's clean hair. Should I change the sheet today? No. It will be just as bad tomorrow. Will Maggie leave me in disgust? No. She was quite put out when I mentioned it. "It'll take more than that to get rid of me!" she said, the doughty girl. I now feel that I have done my Masters in the Quentin Crisp School of Housework.

Once, when I had left home and moved into my own flat, Mum came to visitand, spotting a vase of dead flowers on the mantelpiece, suggested in a worried voice, that I might be "slipping". Mum. There's no doubt now, I've slipped: irredeemably, sartorially (big white cheap cotton knickers, note, potential boyfriends), and domestically.

I've realised, too, that I can trace the genesis of my descent to the time when, as a child, I was taken to visit some aristocratic friends of my parents in a Scottish castle. I had imagined there'd be chandeliers, mile long highly polished banqueting tables, liveried footmen and the like. But we were ushered into a cosy room with a roaring fire, a pile of muddy wellies in the corner, and three old sagging sofas practically upholstered in dogs and so begrimed and chewed and hairy that it was impossible to guess from which Clan of Chintz the family came. Something shifted seismically in my understanding of class and 'classy'. (You mean there is no inviolable moral imperative to keep a clean house?) These people were obviously too posh to push the dogs off the couch and I remember thinking, right then, 'I would like to live like this'.

And so, it seems, I am. If any BBC documentary maker wishes to cast me as A member of a go-back-in-time reality show set in a medieval hovel, be my guest. I have become immune to squalor. And unless (hint hint) Mum buys me the latest Dyson with the Groom Tool Vacuum Assisted Dog Groomer, that's the way it's going to stay.

I wonder if I could sell the hair on eBay?

Dog Ends: An Epidogalogue

Hector is one year old and his birthday passed without ceremony. No, I did not bake him a lamb and chicken-liver birthday cake with an oxo-cube frosting and a tripe stick for a 'candle'. No, I did not take him shopping in Animal House in South Street with my credit card. I didn't even get him a bone. And for reasons mostly pertaining to the August traffic, we missed the birthday gathering of his litter, hosted by his breeder, Jazz, for a celebratory walkies in the New Forest.

Hector's Uncle Murphy was there, and his sister Lexy, his brothers Buster and Samuel, and a cousin Tony (or was that the owner?), Jacob, Miriam. Apparently they all ran up to each other without a single stand-off and started licking each others ears – ah! – before the cow-pat rolling that stood in for musical chairs. How I wished we had been there.

Actually, Hector was suffering from a mysterious bout of fish-breath that dayso I couldn't have privately celebrated his superiority to his siblings to the extent that I had competitively imagined that I might. We stayed in. I did sing Happy Birthday to him. And I went through all his puppy photos and marvelled at how he has grown and how inseparably devoted we have become.

When I was in my twenties I had a vague premonition that my love life would follow the trajectory of Bathsheba Everdene in *Far From the Madding Crowd,* and that after the dashing unfaithful bastard and the stiff-necked father figure and all manner of difficulties, shenanigans and heartbreak, I would end up with Alan Bates, Best Friends Reunited, cosy by the fireside, going, "me fer thee and thee fer me" and all that. Little did I know that my Gabriel Oak would turn out to be a Hector. I am not alone. Most mornings, on the dog-path, a group of us gather at the crossroads by the bridge; Celia and her dogs Patsy and Floyd (once owned by his namesake the great chef himself), and Ivy with her rescue dog Chance ('we gave him a chance and took a chance on him'), and Carol with Chewbacca (Chewy) and her new puppy Yoda, Tanya with Lily, Helen, our esteemed professional dog-walker with her own dog Freddie, and more, converging from each corner of Asker's Meadow like the chorus of a musical or a gaggle of Spanish women meeting to dotheir laundry at the town fountain. Some are widows, most are single, and we gabble on about the weather and our ailments, united by little but our attachment to the dogs who are milling around patiently at our feet. Man's Best Friend? Oh yes, but these days, if we are anything to go by, they are mostly Women's.

Hector is indeed the best friend I have ever had. I don't waste mental space and time on persistent and ungracious speculations about whether he is suffering from an undiagnosed personality disorder. He doesn't gossip about *my* disorders with the other dogs. I can tell him to bugger off without hurting him. Or I can tell him he's the 'boofest of boofs' without him making gagging noises and saying "pass the sick bag". In other words, we love each other without any of the tribulations and disappointments of human friendships.

But I am getting a little bored of writing about us now. What's new? Stop Press! Breaking News! He cocked his leg on a bucket full of flowers in Mum's utility room. He's started scavenging from the kitchen